MIRACLE OR MENACE?

Biotechnology and the Third World

by Robert Walgate

The Panos Institute

Budapest — London — Paris — Washington

Published by Panos Publications Ltd
9 White Lion Street
London N1 9PD, UK

British Library Cataloguing information available.

ISBN 1-870670-18-3

Extracts may be freely reproduced by the press or by non-profit organisations, with or without acknowledgement. Panos would appreciate clippings of published material based on *Miracle or Menace*.

Funding for *Miracle or Menace* was provided by the Rockefeller Foundation, New York and Oxfam, UK.

Any judgments expressed in this document should not be taken to represent the views of any funding agency. Signed articles do not necessarily reflect the views of Panos or any of its funding agencies.

This dossier was written by Robert Walgate, with assistance from: Andy Crump, Talib Esmail, June Goodfield, Khoo Hock Aun, Paul Icamina, K.S. Jayaraman, Bernardo Kolcinski, O'Seun Ogunseitan and Hannah Pearce.
This dossier was edited by Benjamin Pogrund with assistance from Eleanor Lawrence.

The Panos Institute is an international information and policy studies institute, dedicated to working in partnership with others towards greater public understanding of sustainable development. Panos has offices in Budapest, London, Paris and Washington DC and was founded in 1986 by the staff of Earthscan, which had undertaken similar work since 1975.

For more information about Panos contact:
Juliet Heller, The Panos Institute.

Production: Jacqueline Walkden
Picture research: Patricia Lee
Cover design: Viridian
Publications Director: Liz Carlile

Printed in Great Britain by The Southampton Book Company, Southampton

Acknowledgements

It would be impossible to name the tens — hundreds — of individuals who in ways small and large have contributed to this dossier and made it possible. I must begin with the great encouragement given to me by Kenneth Warren, who in his time at the Rockefeller Foundation provided the first pilot grant to begin the project, and Gary Toennissen, also of the Foundation, who continued support and so enabled its completion.

Then must come the many scientists and programme administrators who patiently responded to questioning, and freely provided countless documents, reports and pictures; and then the writers who have contributed excellent material to the dossier from around the world: O'Seun Ogunseitan from Lagos, Bernardo Kolcinski from São Paulo, K.S. Jayaraman from New Delhi, Khoo Hock Aun from Kuala Lumpur, and Paul Icamina from Manila.

In London, Andy Crump helped get the project started; Hannah Pearce, who had worked on biotechnology for Greenpeace, provided her invaluable expertise and energy and researched and wrote the reports on Chinese hybrid rice, cocoa and cassava; June Goodfield generously provided her interview material on rinderpest vaccines; Talib Esmail wrote the rinderpest report and provided much further research and found the excellent pictures.

The dossier would have been impossible without kind invitations to several meetings, such as the European Commission and UN Food and Agriculture Organization's 1989 meeting on Agricultural Biotechnology in Luxembourg, the June 1989 Joint Co-ordinating Board meeting of the UNDP?World Bank/WHO's Tropical Disease Research Programme in Geneva, and the Rockefeller Foundation's Rice Biotechnology Programme annual meeting in 1989 in Columbia, Missouri.

Last but not least, I shall have undying gratitude to my editors, Benjamin Pogrund for his unfailing sense of clear English, rejection of obscurity — and willingness to learn some molecular biology! — and the untiring and painstaking Eleanor Lawrence, who going far beyond the call of contract and duty has ensured that the text is short, to the point, and scientifically as accurate as can be achieved in the time and space available to us; to Liz Carlile, who has ensured that the book was not only produced, but looked good too, against constant changes of deadlines by a pressing author; to James Deane for helping to find the funds for publication; and to Jon Tinker for having the foresight to let me undertake this project.

In the end, though, the responsibility must be mine. Any errors of judgment, fact or balance, must be laid at my door.

Robert Walgate
London
May 1990

Preface

Technology has transformed the lives of nearly everyone on the planet. Automobiles, corrugated iron, plastic shoes, calculators, fertilisers, jumbo jets, television, tractors, nuclear weapons...

The twentieth century so far has been dominated by technologies based on physics and chemistry. Now it is biology's turn. Biotechnology, the application of an explosion of biological knowledge over the last twenty years, gives humankind the ability to alter the structure of life itself.

The risks and the benefits of biotechnology are similar to those offered by any new technology: electricity, the microchip or chemical fertiliser. Who controls it, and for whose benefit?

The potential of biotechnology is enormous. In 1885 Louis Pasteur developed the first vaccine — against rabies. Since then, 21 other effective vaccines have been developed against human diseases. With the help of biotechnology another 28 may be produced over the next decade, which could have bigger impacts on human health than the introduction of antibiotics.

Biotechnology can telescope years of laborious plant or animal breeding into a few hours of genetic manipulation, offering the prospect of massive increases in food and crop production at a time when human populations are still rising steadily, and when global food stocks have rarely looked more precarious.

For the West, biotechnology may well bring further increases in affluence. For the Third World, it could bring less hunger and starvation — or more; less disease and sickness — or more; better or — perhaps even worse — standards of living.

In the 1960s and 1970s, new high-yielding varieties of rice and wheat, combined with effective pesticides and chemical fertilisers, dramatically increased food production in some of the poorest countries of the world. For some people, the Green Revolution raised living standards substantially, but it also forced many of the poorer farmers to sell their land to those rich enough to invest quickly in the new technology. In some countries, economic inequality, and consequent political and social tensions, were greatly increased.

Biotechnology will pose many similar problems. It is now possible to manipulate the genetic make-up of a crop so that it is resistant to a specific weedkiller. Farmers who buy these new varieties should be able to achieve much higher yields — but only if they also buy the appropriate weedkiller. If the new technology is only available to the richer farmers, poverty and inequality may be deepened.

For the technologies based on physics and chemistry, most of the Third World has been a bystander, receiving leftovers from western tables, with little opportunity to influence research or innovation. With biotechnology too, the West, mainly through new multinational companies, is already defining the direction and emphases of research and development. Yet there are many biotechnology research institutes in the South, both private and public, which could play a key role in ensuring that biotechnology benefits the Third World as well as the industrialised North.

Much of the biological wealth on which biotechnological research depends is found in the Third World. The biotechnology industry needs the genes from plants and animals, yeasts and bacteria which can still be found in the forests and wildernesses of the developing world. This could provide a way for the poorer nations of the world to have, if not a controlling interest, at least a substantial shareholding in the future direction of biotechnological research.

Biotechnology raises profound economic, environmental and political questions — and fierce and often ill-informed passions. This dossier explains some of the promises offered by biotechnology, especially to the Third World, and outlines some of the risks and dangers associated with it. Whether biotechnology proves to be a miracle or a menace depends on how it is used and controlled.

But control depends upon knowledge, and biotechnology is such a new subject that even science graduates often have only a sketchy understanding of it. The Panos Institute hopes that this publication will help stimulate and inform a debate both in the North and in the South, on how biotechnology can best be harnessed in the service of humankind — and on how we can ensure that biotechnology is used to reduce rather than to deepen the obscene inequities which exist today both between and within different countries.

Jon Tinker
President
The Panos Institute.

CONTENTS

BOXED INFORMATION

A few basics, 2 — Recombinant DNA, 3 — Species, varieties, lines, 10 — Tissue culture, 12 — Malaysia to clone rattan, 25 — Vietnam's success with potatoes, 29 — Plant cells, 31 — Bananas and plantains, 35 — DNA cloning, 42 — Gene 'expression', 44 — Viruses, 49 — DNA probes, 53 — Kenya smallholders win out, 67 — Human gene therapy, 72 — DNA sequencing, 74 — Vaccines, 80 — Antigens and antibodies, 92 — The malaria parasite, 99 — Bacterial protein factories, 109 — Blue-green algae in India, 121 — Transgenic animals, 127 — Improving Indian cattle, 128 — Free drug to halt river blindness, 137 — Mary's DNA fingerprint, 155 — Thaumatin brings riches only to some, 161

CHAPTER 1

TAKING CONTROL OF EVOLUTION

Biologists can now control the molecular basis of life. With this control, they have the power to transform the world.

They will do this through *biotechnology* — the application of biological science to the manipulation and use of living things for human ends.

Biotechnology is creating dramatic new opportunities for the scientific manipulation of micro-organisms, plants and animals: a new level of control of the biosphere which, for the Third World, could both help and hinder development.

The Third World is a biological world. Most of the world's staple crops first grew there. Most of the world's parasites, insects, pests, plants and creatures of all kinds flourish there. Third World economies are heavily dependent on biological products: most earnings come from biological commodities such as sugar, cocoa, timber or cotton.

Now, in agriculture, whole markets will vanish, and new ones will appear, as new products are developed and traditional ones superseded — creating new forms of economic advantage and disadvantage. For example, the yield of cassava, the staple food crop in much of Africa, could be quadrupled if the plant could be made resistant to one of its main diseases — African cassava mosaic virus. On the other hand, vanilla pods, the main export of Madagascar, could be wiped out if biotechnologists succeed in creating a bacterium that could make vanillin, the molecule that gives the flavour of vanilla, in a factory fermenter.

In health, biotechnology heralds a new era of Third World preventative and curative medicine. For example, if the funding and researchers can be found, and provided research programmes are appropriately directed to real Third World need, biotechnology promises effective vaccines over the next decade for another 28 diseases, from malaria to leprosy next decade — a more than ten-fold increase in the rate of vaccine development.

Biotechnology itself is not new. For thousands of years, people have used yeast and other microbes to ferment food, brew beer and

A FEW BASICS

● Living organisms such as plants and animals are made up of millions of individual cells – tiny living building blocks.
● Each cell contains a set of biological instructions – the genes. All the cells of any one organism carry an identical set of genes.
● Each gene spells out just one of the many thousands of instructions needed to build and maintain a living organism.
● The genes of a life-form determine what it looks like and what it can do – for example, what chemicals it can make, what diseases it is resistant to, the food quality of its seeds, roots or leaves.
● Finding and transferring genes between interbreeding species, by crossing two plants or two animals, is the basis of traditional plant or animal breeding. But the methods are slow and laborious, and limited to species which will mate.
● Over the past 15 years, geneticists have learnt how to snip out an individual gene from the cells of one species of living thing, and insert it into the cells of another species. This is genetic engineering.
● The first genetically engineered organisms were single-celled bacteria, into which human genes for valuable products such as insulin (for diabetics) or human growth hormone (for children whose growth is severely retarded) had been transplanted. The bacteria were then able to manufacture these useful proteins in large amounts.
● Genetically engineered plants and animals soon followed, opening up the whole field of agriculture to the new biotechnology.

leaven bread. In this century, biotechnology has provided mass-produced antibiotics and vaccines.

But over the past 10 years, revolutionary advances in the basic sciences of genetics and biochemistry have vastly increased the potential power of biotechnology and enlarged the scope of its activities.

The powerful new tool of biotechnology is *genetic engineering*, and the associated *recombinant DNA technology* that makes it possible. These techniques give humankind the ability to create novel plants, animals, and micro-organisms with properties they could never have acquired naturally.

With this new-found control over the *genes* — the biological instructions that determine what any living organism looks like and what it can do — the evolution of life has become a conscious process. New organisms are now being created not according to the natural laws of survival, but according to human will. The results will inevitably be profound: they may be destructive; they may be creative. They will probably be both.

The real impact of biotechnology will be determined by two key factors:

•   Who steers the research programmes, and to what ends.

A FEW BASICS... recombinant DNA

● Genes are made of DNA (deoxyribonucleic acid), an extraordinary molecule which encodes biological instructions in its chemical structure.

● The chemical structure of DNA is like a string of letters, spelling out the genetic message. The letters – there are only four in the genetic alphabet – are called bases.

● Each gene consists of a stretch of DNA many thousands of bases long.

● Genes are carried on the chromosomes of a cell. Each chromosome contains a single, very long DNA molecule, millions of bases long, which encodes many genes along its length.

● DNA is easily extracted from cells, and advances in molecular biology now allow scientists to snip out individual genes from the DNA of one species and make them molecular constructs – recombinant DNAs – that can be stored indefinitely in the laboratory. The gene can then be retrieved if needed for some genetic engineering application. Genes isolated in this way are called cloned genes.

● How far public and democratic processes can influence those who steer the programmes.

In the present world economy, the outcome might seem obvious: biotechnology will be for the rich North, whose major companies already control most of the key technologies and aim to turn them into sizeable profits.

However, biotechnology is infinitely flexible, and could be turned to the needs of the South, provided the appropriate research and development programmes are established. For example, why has cassava not yet been transformed and improved? Largely, because the owners of the necessary techniques see no profit to be made from it.

There is much room for pro-South publicly funded research into such problems; and even private industry may be prepared to help if the work boosts the company image and does not affect profits elsewhere.

The real challenge, therefore, is to identify biotechnological research

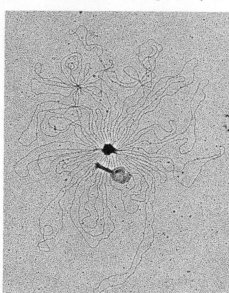

Threads of DNA, the molecule that controls life and inheritance, spill from the broken head of a virus. The genetic engineers power to control DNA is a power to control life. /J. Meyer/ Biozentrum,University of Basel/Science Photo Library

Rural farmer in Africa: to improve her lot, biotechnology planning must be localised, responsible and sophisticated.
/Ron Giling/Panos Pictures

that would be appropriate to development — in particular, to improving the lot of the poorest communities — and to get that research effectively funded and managed.

Even "appropriate" research is no panacea: it can go awry in many ways. Biotechnology must take into account real need — which means asking farmers what they require, rather than delivering advanced technology from above that may not be wanted. And it should not over-sell. The promise of an early vaccine for malaria led to huge research funds from the United States Army, which was interested in protecting troops abroad. But the early promise soon vanished, as the problem turned out to be more complex than had been thought, leaving disillusion and recriminations in its wake.

Public influence over biotechnology, to shift its programme to the problems that concern the developing world, requires that the technology be properly understood. There must be understanding of what biotechnology can and cannot deliver. To explain these matters, and the issues surrounding them, in the context of developing country concerns, is the purpose of this dossier.

The dossier is designed to:

- **Clarify** the basic science behind biotechnology.

- **Tackle controversies** over the possible risks and benefits of biotechnology for the poor.

- **Report stories** — actual cases of applications, research programmes and policies.

It aims to be useful to several groups of readers: to journalists and non-governmental organisations wishing to report or campaign on these issues in their own countries; to policy-makers planning research spending in biotechnologies which are intended to aid development; to biotechnologists who would like to improve their understanding of development issues, and perhaps take directions in their research that might be more appropriate to the disadvantaged three-quarters of the world's population; to development professionals who would like to improve their understanding of biotechnology; and to the general reader.

The basic biology necessary to understand biotechnology is presented in small doses, in boxes, throughout the text, both here and in later chapters. A more detailed description, for those who wish it, is given in the Appendix.

Chapters 2 to 4 cover the main biotechnologies affecting crop plants, with several examples, including an emphasis on rice — whose production must grow by nearly half by the year 2000 to meet world population growth. Chapter 5 looks in more detail at the potential impact of biotechnology on three crops: cacao, cassava and trees.

Chapter 6 deals with the increasing role of biotechnology in medicine, and identifies research needs in the South, while Chapter 7 looks more closely at the scientific rationale behind the design of new vaccines and drugs and their possible impact on three major diseases, malaria, Chagas' disease and leprosy. Chapter 8 looks at the use and genetic engineering of microbes, Chapter 9 describes biotechnology's impacts on the use of animals.

Chapter 10 deals with issues of private power and public interest, with a special report on the US private ownership of techniques for developing hybrid rice that originated in China. Chapter 11 deals with genetic resources and the claim of "farmers' rights"; and Chapter 12 with environmental issues. Chapter 13 offers conclusions.

CHAPTER 2

FINDING GENES FOR BETTER CROPS

THE PROBLEM

For every person in the affluent North, one person is close to starvation in the poor South — which means 700 million hungry people [1]. More than 500 million of them live in the rural areas of the lowest-income countries, with per capita incomes of under US$400 a year in 1983. The rest cluster in shanty towns around urban areas.

Latin America has some 70 million hungry; Africa has double that, with 140 million; and South Asia, including India, 350 million.

The Green Revolution — the boost in food production provided by the development of high-yielding dwarf wheats and rices, grown on some of the best lands in the developing countries since the 1960s — can no longer cope with the increased demand for food from a rising population. Total yields appear to be reaching their peak. During the past three decades, these crops have increased world food production by 50 billion tonnes a year [2], and so far have kept food supply in step with population growth.

The Green Revolution crops were bred to give high yields under good conditions. In particular, they are more responsive to fertiliser than the old "farmers' varieties", and are more uniform and consistent in quality. However, they need reasonably good soils, and ample water, and expensive fertiliser and pesticides to be successful. Most suitable land is now planted with these crops and the long period of growth in the world food supply seems to be ending.

Rice, for example, provides half the total calorie intake for 2 billion people, and in some areas of Asia it provides 70% of the protein in the diet. But China is approaching the limits of rice yield using available agricultural technology. Indian rice production also appears to be levelling off. Globally, population projections indicate that rice production must increase by 45% this decade.

The long-term solution to the food supply problem can only be fewer people — but that is an impossible goal in the short or even medium term. The only short-term solution is more food.

Food aid saves lives. But it is not the best answer for long-term food supply in developing countries. This is a feeding programme with US surplus grain in Burkina Faso. /*Sean Sprague/Panos Pictures*

Where is this food to come from?

Food aid from over-productive countries cannot meet demand, and in itself hinders Third World agricultural development. The burden of raising food production and alleviating hunger must be shouldered elsewhere. Politicians and economists have had little success. That leaves the agricultural sciences to produce more yield and reduce losses to pests and diseases. And increasingly that means the use of biotechnology: the leading edge of plant science.

With the help of biotechnology and genetic engineering, increased food production could come from finding and using new genes for:

* **Increasing the resistance of high-yielding modern crop varieties to pests and disease, and extending their ability to thrive in harsher conditions.**

Some 20-40% of the world's agricultural production is lost due to pests, weeds and diseases. World spending on pesticides has reached US$16 billion a year — US$3 for every person on Earth. Yet some 500 insects have already developed substantial levels of resistance to insecticides [3]. Plant breeders are on a treadmill, continually turning out novel crop varieties to beat insects and diseases which evolve — often quite rapidly — to colonise and destroy each new variety.

The unconventional techniques of plant biotechnology are

providing new routes to breeding-in disease and pest resistances not previously available to the plant breeder.

- **Increasing the productivity of crops grown in marginal lands.**

The majority of hungry people — around two-thirds — live in marginal lands with poor soil and uncertain rainfall, areas never reached by the water-, pesticide- and fertiliser-demanding Green Revolution crops. Whereas the Green Revolution required alteration of the environment to suit the crop (such as demanding dams for irrigation and large applications of chemicals), biotechnology offers alteration of the crop to suit the environment [4].

- **Improving certain food and cash crops that have proved resistant to conventional plant breeding.**

Some plants, including many trees and shrubs, take years to come to maturity and flower, or rarely set seed, so conventional breeding can take decades or be quite impossible. Ways of inducing early flowering, so that many more seedlings can be produced, are now being developed.

Where should the effort go?

The Green Revolution seems to have passed by a substantial minority of the world's hungry who actually live in the world's agri- culturally more productive areas, such as the plains of the Ganges and Brahmaputra in India, and the Kenyan highlands in Africa. At the same time, critics of the Green Revolution argue that, although it bought un-parallelled increases in food production, the benefits of such increases were felt mainly by the rich farmers — they by-passed the poor.

Arguably, land reform could bring the most immediate benefits in these areas, but, politically, it is often difficult to achieve. Bangladesh, for example, may struggle with land reform — but it could do much more with science, if only it had the funds and the researchers to breed enough high-yielding, disease-resistant rice varieties suited to its frequently flooded and saline conditions.

The International Food Policy Research Institute in Washington DC identifies a wide research gap even in Green Revolution areas. The institute recommends that researchers concentrate on improving productivity in these already highly productive lands, as it believes total food production can be increased fastest where the work is easiest [5].

On the other hand, almost no significant agricultural science or technology at all has penetrated to those people living in marginal lands, such as much of upland India and the Sahel in Africa. Some commentators are sceptical that it ever will — at least in the short term — but for the more optimistic an enormous task lies ahead.

Maize in Kenya affected by streak virus. /*Nigel Cattlin/Holt Studios Ltd*

Given the potential power and precision of biotechnology to deliver a particular product, the most immediate aim is to define appropriate research goals fitted closely to the relevant area, and to pursue them rapidly. Help will also be needed to provide the necessary infrastructure to deliver any results.

One goal of appropriate biotechnological research, in both the best and the marginal lands, must be to aim at food self-sufficiency. Another related aim will be to increase the income of the poor, so that city dwellers and agricultural labourers can buy food. This will allow food farmers to make agriculturally productive investments; for example, to improve food storage or buy fertiliser.

Biotechnology's role in income generation could be two-fold: to improve existing cash crops and develop new uses for them; and to generate entirely new forms of income for developing countries, based on establishing their ownership and control over the vast resources of genetic material locked in their fields and forests.

PLANT BREEDING

In immediate practical terms, what can biotechnology do for agriculture?

Its first and most fundamental contribution will be to *speed up plant breeding*, so improving traditional gene transfer methods.

Plant breeding is often excruciatingly slow. For example, the three most important characteristics of European sugar-beet — its high sugar yield, its resistance to "bolting" (growing too thin and fast), and its production of a single-seeded fruit, which aids mechanised planting — took a quarter century to select, breed in, and distribute to farmers.

This slow pace is partly the inevitable result of the long time needed for the many cycles of crossing, growing to maturity, back-crossing with the parents, and so on, to transfer genes for desirable characters while eliminating undesirable ones.

In the genetic lottery, crossing a high-yielding, but disease-prone, plant with a less productive but disease-resistant plant, does not always give a high-yielding, disease-resistant offspring. Depending on the exact genetic make-up of the parents it is just as likely to produce a preponderance of low-yielding, disease-prone offspring.

The offspring will usually be quite variable, differing both from their parents and from each other, just as children of the same parents are never identical to each other (except for identical twins) or to their parents.

Plant breeders have to put their plants through repeated rounds of interbreeding, which can sometimes take years, before they can come up with useful breeding lines that contain the genes they want, and that will transmit them in a reasonably predictable manner.

Even so, plant breeders have contributed more than half of the five- to ten-fold increase in agricultural yields over the last 50 years; the rest has come from improved agricultural practice and machinery, fertilisers, weedkillers, and pesticides [6].

Plant breeding for developing countries now has some formidable

A FEW BASICS... species, varieties, lines

● Plants and animals come in a vast variety of different sorts – or species. The simple biological definition of a species is that members of the same species can interbreed among themselves but cannot breed with the members of any other species.

● Each species has been given a double-barrelled Latin name consisting, first, of a surname (or generic name) which may be shared with other closely related species, followed by the specific name, which tells exactly what species it is. Bread wheat, for example, is *Triticum aestivum* whereas rye is *Triticum secale*. Rice is *Oryza sativa*.

● Within some species – especially of crop plants or domesticated animals – there are many varieties. A variety of plant or animal is genetically different in some respect from other varieties of the same species, but will still interbreed with them. Among bread wheats, for example, there are many varieties that consistently differ in their resistance to certain diseases, their height, their yield potential, the "hardness" of the grain and so on.

● A particular line of a crop plant is a pure-breeding variety. Two plants of the same line when crossed will always produce a plant with the same characteristics as the parents.

hurdles to cross.

The only way to increase the productivity of high-yielding varieties of, say, wheat and rice in the good lands, is now to make them more resistant to common pests and diseases. Pesticides cost money, as well as being environmentally damaging in many cases. Inbuilt long-lasting genetic resis-

Banana plantation in Thailand wrecked by fungal attack./*Nigel Cattlin/Holt Studios Ltd*

tance to disease is the long-term goal of the plant breeder. But it is very difficult to achieve. Genes for disease and pest resistance are hard to find, and often exist only in wild and weedy relatives of the crop plant, or in some other even more distantly related species.

The other aim is to extend the areas which can be planted to modern high-yielding crops. Many marginal lands are too dry for Green Revolution wheats, for example, although they can support older indigenous varieties. Natural soil conditions or bad irrigation practice over many years mean that much soil is too salty, lacks essential minerals, or is too full of other harmful minerals to support many modern crop varieties. First, the plant breeder must find genes that confer resistance to harsh conditions such as salinity and drought. Then these genes must be transferred into useful modern varieties.

Genes for stress resistance are again more likely to be found in wild and weedy relatives of crop plants, or in the old farmers' varieties. Transferring genes from one species to another is difficult by conventional plant breeding, as two different species do not naturally interbreed successfully. The less closely related the species, the more difficult it is to get even a very rare successful cross.

Even where two varieties will crossbreed easily, conventional crossing is not always the most efficient way of constructing a new variety. Many desirable characteristics are determined by many genes acting together. Because of the nature of sexual reproduction, crossing can only bring some of these genes over into the hybrid (each parent transmits only half of its total gene set to the offspring). Thus useful combinations of genes tend to get separated, and as breeding proceeds, disease resistance or other desirable characters tend to become weaker, as some of the useful genes are lost.

A FEW BASICS... tissue culture

● As well as reproducing by seeds (so-called sexual reproduction), many plants can also reproduce themselves vegetatively. For example, a complete new plant can often be grown from a detached piece of root, shoot or leaf. In this case, the resulting new plants are genetically identical to their parent.

● Plants (and all other organisms) grow by cell division. Cells grow to a certain size and then divide into two. When a cell divides, the genes it contains also duplicate themselves, so that an identical set is inherited by each new cell.

● So all the cells arising from a single cell are genetically identical to it, and a plant that grows from a single cell or a small piece of cultured plant tissue is therefore genetically identical to the parent plant from which the tissue came.

● This is the basis of plant cloning, or micro-propagation of plants in tissue culture.

Tissue culture and genetic engineering

As described in more detail in the next two chapters, biotechnology offers greater control and precision in determining which genes will be transferred, and also makes the task of transferring genes between different species much quicker and easier. Plant tissue culture (Chapter 3) and plant genetic engineering (Chapter 4), potentially offer breeders the chance to leap some of their hurdles.

Tissue culture — growing small pieces of plant tissue or individual plant cells in culture, and propagating many new identical plants from them — is the real basis of plant biotechnology.

It makes possible:

- Large-scale, speedy propagation of "elite" varieties by making many "clones", or identical copies, of a plant. This avoids the genetic variability that arises in crossbreeding.

- Crosses between distantly related species, by fusing cells of the two species in tissue culture to produce a hybrid cell from which a new hybrid plant can be grown.

- Easier international exchange of plant material, by providing disease-free material grown in tissue culture using parts of the plant that remain free of disease.

- More ways of conserving and storing a wide variety of plant germplasm — the material such as seeds or tissue cultures from which new plants can be grown. Within any species of plant (or animal) there is considerable genetic variation from individual to individual. This reflects the fact that many genes exist in several different forms within the population as a whole. It is this variation that the plant breeder works with, and it must be conserved for the future. So much variation has already disappeared or is fast disappearing, both from the wild and from farmers' fields, as genetically uniform crop varieties replace the older, more diverse farmers' varieties.

Storage of plant germplasm as frozen tissue cultures will be particularly useful for plants that produce only poor seed, or produce it rarely, or in a difficult form for mass storage — such as coconut.

Tissue culture also offers the prospect of greatly speeding up the improvement of long-lived trees and shrubs, among which are many useful food and cash crops such as plantains, coffee and oil palm. Woody plants often take years to grow to maturity, flower and set seed, but elite plants of at least some species can now be propagated from tissue cultures, and also be induced to flower much sooner in tissue culture.

Genetic engineering and its associated techniques is a much newer technology, and has yet to show its full potential. Already it can offer:

- New biochemical methods of quickly detecting whether a certain gene is present in a plant. These sorts of tests, used to screen seedlings early in a plant breeding programme, can save valuable time and money in planting out and screening much later at maturity.

- Techniques for extracting a gene from virtually any species — not necessarily another plant — and transferring it into plant cells in culture, from which a genetically novel plant can be grown.

- Techniques for altering genes in the test-tube, before replacing them in their original cell or a new host cell.

Plant breeders can, in principle, now take useful genes from anywhere across the whole kingdom of life, insert them into crop plants and grow a transgenic crop with the new gene. Tomato and tobacco plants now exist, for example, carrying genes transferred from viruses (to protect them from virus disease) and

Transporting millet in Niger — a valuable, but under-researched, arid-land crop. /*Ron Giling/Panos Pictures* bacteria (to produce insect-killing toxins).

Tissue culture and genetic engineering techniques combined are expected to halve the time it usually takes to develop a new variety.

But before genetic engineering can be widely used by plant breeders there must be more work on:

- Finding suitable genes to transfer, in whatever organisms they may be.

- Learning more about which genes determine which characters in plants.

- Making detailed genetic "maps" for each species, showing which genes are located on which chromosomes, and the order in which they occur on the chromosomes. Comprehensive gene maps make it much easier to find and extract a gene.

- Perfecting techniques of gene transfer for many more species of plant than at present.

More than just science is needed

Breeding new crops is not just a scientific exercise. Molecular biotechnologists will have to work very closely with plant breeders, and plant breeders with farmers at the grassroots, if genetic improvements are to be bred not just into experimental varieties, but into local crops of real importance for the rural areas and the urban poor of developing countries.

For example, in Africa, researchers developed an "improved" sorghum with high yield — but farmers would not use it. The scientists had not realised, or had not taken the trouble to find out, that the farmers used the stems to make roofs for their homes; and the stem of the "improved" variety was too short to make good thatch [7].

If developing countries are to exploit fully the opportunities offered by biotechnology at lease four fundamental elements appear to be necessary:

- **Effective mechanisms** to assess real needs.

- **Skill in tissue culture**, the essential basic biotechnology for plants.

- **An established infrastructure for plant breeding**, presently lacking in many developing countries.

- **Regulations** to investigate and control risks.

  And for the full use of the technologies:

- **Skill in molecular biology** and genetic engineering, present

Hausa man in Niger harvesting sorghum — another key, but under-researched, food crop for arid lands. /*Ron Giling/Panos Pictures*

in only a few developing countries and generally requiring collaboration with research groups in the industrialised world.

- **Agreements on recognition** of Northern patents and plant breeders' rights (to allow access to advanced private company technologies, where much present expertise resides), in exchange for recognition of developing countries' "farmers' rights" (see Chapter 9).

FOCUS ON THREE NATIONS

Indonesia, Zimbabwe and Mexico offer good examples of how developing countries in Asia, Africa and Latin America are attempting to make use of biotechnology for plant breeding. Indonesia plans a major programme on its staple food, rice; Zimbabwe is interested in the African staple, cassava — as well as several other locally important crops such as tobacco; and Mexico, which each year loses half its citrus crop to disease, aims to use biotechnology to protect that crop, and to improve the fibre plant, henequen.

Indonesia: Tripling of rice production is not enough

The further planting of Green Revolution rice in Indonesia will not be enough to keep up with a growing population, expected to reach 216

million in 2000. Rice production must grow another 40% in the next 10 years for the country to maintain self-sufficiency.

So rice biotechnology will be applied "to produce new superior rice crop plants more quickly than by conventional methods," says Ibrahim Manwan, director of the Indonesian Central Research Institute for Food Crops.

According to Manwan and his co-researcher, M. Fatchurochim Masyhudi [8], biotechnology "is expected to... bring major breakthroughs for production increases". Consequently, Indonesia has established The Bogor Research Institute for Food Crops to develop this biotechnology for Indonesia. Its research programme includes:

- Use of tissue culture and cell fusion to speed gene transfer and breeding of new rice lines.

- Use of biotechnical methods to identify useful genes in breeding lines.

- Development of high-yielding lines of rice adapted to the various agro-ecological zones of Indonesia, with resistance to local pests and physical stresses.

- Basic research to improve information and methods for pest identification and control.

- Research on soil micro-organisms and their interaction with plant roots to improve nitrogen and phosphorus uptake.

- Development of methods to convert crop residues into useful fertiliser.

Zimbabwe: Planning a biotech institute

The University of Zimbabwe has been planning a new biotechnology institute, needing US$5 million over five years [9]. According to Dr Ian Robertson, of the university's Department of Crop Science, its goals would be to develop a "critical mass" of scientists "paid a good enough salary to keep the team stable over 10 years".

The research would require the techniques of cell and tissue culture, regeneration techniques (growing single cells into plants), the insertion of foreign genes into cells, the construction of the molecular tools for genetic engineering, the selection of "gene regulators" (pieces of DNA that set genes to work, turning them "on" and "off") and carefully monitored laboratory, greenhouse and field trials.

In order of the ease of the methods now available, and so in order of likely success, it would focus on developing:

- Cassava resistant to African cassava mosaic virus.

- Sweet potato resistant to poti virus.

- Cowpea resistant to Maruka disease.

- Tobacco resistant to herbicides, tobacco mosaic virus and budworm.

- Cotton resistant to pink bollworm.

- Tomato resistant to mosaic virus.

- Maize resistant to stem-borers.

- Groundnut resistant to groundnut rosette assis virus.

- Coffee resistant to coffee-berry disease.

Mexico: Half the citrus crop lost to disease

The Yucatan peninsula — a neglected, agriculturally impoverished region of Mexico — grows crops such as citrus and henequen, which were totally unaffected by the Green Revolution, but which are of critical importance for the poor. Could biotechnology help? So ask Amarella Eastmond and Manuel L. Robert in a study prepared for the International Labour Organization [10].

Their answer? Yes, under certain conditions:

- If biotechnology could help save the 50% of the Yucatan citrus crop that is lost to pests and diseases each year. Any loss in labour requirement for pest and weed control (if biopesticides or resistant citrus varieties were available) would be compensated by the extra labour required for harvesting and transporting the greater output.

- If biotechnology could improve henequen. Nearly a quarter of the Yucatan labour force depend on henequen — a fibre like sisal used for ropes — for their work, though production has been falling for years. To increase labour opportunities, henequen could be made more productive, the fibre quality improved to compete better on world markets, and elite varieties cloned and propagated.

- If biotechnology could reduce the need for expensive pesticide treatment of coffee against leaf rust. Coffee is Mexico's main agricultural export and second only to oil. The livelihoods of 93,000 small producers — accounting for three-quarters of the total — depend on the crop. Reduced labour use in spraying would be compensated by increased use in processing an increased crop.

- If biotechnology could control "lethal yellowing", a coconut disease now spreading in Mexico that kills palms within five months of the first symptoms appearing. If the disease were halted, some 800,000 hectares of Mexico could be planted to coconut to provide rural employment.

FOCUS ON RICE RESEARCH

Rice — Asia's main food staple — is benefiting from intensive research interest among molecular biologists, not only in the South, but also among the universities of the industrialised world.

Why? First, because compared with other cereals, rice has relatively few genes, so genetic engineers and breeders are able to find their way around those genes with relative ease. Second, because the Rockefeller Foundation — which inspired the Green Revolution — decided to pull out the stops and set up an international rice biotechnology programme to co-ordinate and fund the research that was needed. And third, because the International Rice Research Institute (IRRI) in the Philippines, which was one of the first of the 13 International Agricultural Research Centres set up by the Rockefeller Foundation to deal with developing country crops, and which was a prime mover in the Green Revolution, is turning its attention to the use of biotechnology, and to the needs of marginal farmers.

The Rockefeller Foundation Rice Biotechnology Programme

To prepare its own rice biotechnology programme, the Rockefeller Foundation developed a detailed list of research priorities, combining questions of need and biotechnical feasibility, and then set about putting together a team of rice biotechnologists, North and South, to add to the few pioneers already at work.

They came willingly. One leading US biotechnologist, when asked why she had turned to rice biotechnology, said realistically, "because the money was offered... Every problem in biology is interesting, and you work where the grants are." Others feel the same. It is clear that if donors put money into important biological problems that affect the South, then scientists will follow.

Results have come extremely fast (some are described in this dossier), bringing rice to the stage where it is poised to become the model cereal for biotechnology experiments. Now rice seems set to stay on the research agenda even if Rockefeller's research funds are withdrawn [11].

The proof of this, however, will only come when new improved rices, useful in developing country conditions, are produced through the programme. This will take time. The most immediate, practical applications of rice biotechnology are mostly likely to come from:

- A map of the rice genes being developed at Cornell University, in the United States, to help researchers and breeders find the genes they need. This will speed the identification and breeding-in of useful characteristics, which is carried out at the international and national rice breeding centres.

For example, the soils of the acidic uplands and lowlands of India are affected by aluminium and iron. Some local rice plants can tolerate the metals, and, in Hyderabad, geneticists are using genetic maps to study the genes causing that tolerance, with the aim of introducing them into agriculturally more useful varieties.

- The use of tissue culture techniques which greatly accelerate breeding and enable breeders to cross good but delicate rices with wild — but hardy — relatives.

The top seven application priorities of the programme, taking into account both the impact that problems with rice can have on poverty, and the probable ease of their solution by biotechnology, are:

- Tungro virus.
- Yellow stem-borer (an insect).

- Gall midge (an insect).
- Rice "cytoplasmic male sterility" (enabling the breeding of hybrid rices with typically 25% more yield).
- Upland rice: drought resistance, blast fungus resistance, and tolerance of soil iron deficiency.
- Brown plant-hopper (an insect).
- Tolerance of submergence (flash floods).

Together, these cause losses valued by the Rockefeller Foundation at over US$7 billion.

Robert Herdt, director of the foundation's agricultural department, was asked to define these priorities. "We got together a bunch of well-travelled rice scientists, who'd seen many farmers, and went through some intensive questioning on the percentages of areas affected by what problems," he said.

"At the same time, we identified what might be achieved with biotechnology. We asked how long it might take to achieve a given target. Drought resistances looked 15 years off, but transgenic rice with virus resistance might be only three years away. Then we calculated the investment required for each target."

The basic goals in the foundation's programme are to build biotechnology capacity in developing countries, and to create improved varieties of rice.

"We need a co-operative relationship between people who work daily with farmers, and the biologists," said Herdt.

Farmers in developing countries are eager to adopt new varieties — where they are applicable, he noted. For example, in the Green Revolution, farmers were prepared to increase fertiliser inputs ten-fold from 5 to 50 kilograms per hectare, to farm the high-yielding dwarf varieties.

But, according to John O'Toole, the Rockefeller Foundation's representative in New Delhi, Indian growers are mostly interested in what biotechnology can do to increase their incomes in export markets — for example, by producing better aromatic rices like Basmati: "They are not interested in equity."

Meanwhile, said Herdt, the programme is doing well with developing resistance to rice tungro virus, insects and rice blast fungus; but not so well with gall midge, tolerance to drought (and flooding), and some other diseases.

But "there must be additional research on biosafety and ecological impacts... Scientists must be prepared to serve on advisory and regulatory commissions... and there is going to have to be public education."

IRRI: Towards the year 2000

At the same time, the giant, 2,500-scientist, International Rice Research Institute (IRRI) in Manila in the Philippines, has been planning its new five-year research programme [12].

IRRI's research will be divided into four projects focused on distinct eco-agricultural rice areas (irrigated rice, rainfed lowland rice, upland rice, and deep-water and tidal wetland rice); and a fifth "cross-eco-system" project, spending 35% of IRRI's resources, in which the biotechnology work will fall.

"We are getting our scientists to focus on the way rice is grown," said Hubert G. Zandstra, IRRI's deputy director-general for research. Rice ecologists are joining with the scientists in a "multidisciplinary ecosystem approach". Out of 60 senior scientists at IRRI, five are now socio-economics experts, Zandstra said.

Does the programme address the problems of the poorest communities, who are often living on the worst land?

According to Zandstra, over the last decade each ecosystem has been examined for "real problems" — "so local issues are well-represented". However, he said it was "quite rare" that a technology could be found to reduce relative poverty between groups.

Planning the IRRI programme took five years. "Step one was interest-group analysis — looking at owners, the landless, labour, women, tenants, scientists and policy-makers — to see how local constraints and resources could be alleviated or improved by research," said Zandstra.

How did IRRI ensure that developments would be acceptable to and used by its client communities?

"These questions of constraints and acceptability — it's a very precise art, like trying to hit 10 bulls' eyes at once," he said. "Some technologies are robust, and get widely adopted; others need to be 'fine-tuned' to suit farmers' needs. IRRI is now involved in much 'adjustment research'.

"We planned the programme by looking at our clients [the farming families], and doing a 'problem tree analysis' and inverting it... we got down to 47 useful projects from our previous 90. For example, we found pest management was more of a problem for irrigated rice than for upland or rainfed rice. So we cut our pest programmes in the latter areas."

IRRI's goal in irrigated rice — the bulk of rice production — is to increase and at least maintain the yield. This requires continuous maintenance as pests evolve around the barriers put up by breeders and agrochemicals.

IRRI is using tissue culture to speed the breeding of cold-, salt-, aluminium- and disease-tolerant rice varieties, and rice for upland conditions. Hybrids, which normally have to be produced each season by crossing the parent varieties, are being multiplied by anther culture (see Chapter 3) to produce 50-100 plants from every cross. These are being distributed to national research programmes for selection for tolerance to various important local stresses.

CHAPTER 3

PLANT TISSUE CULTURE

B efore biotechnology can have any impact on a plant, the plant must be amenable to being grown in tissue culture, which rapidly multiplies all the genes of a single plant at once (see box page 2).

Tissue culture is a two-edged sword. It can bring developing countries great benefits, particularly in plant breeding and multiplication of elite plants; but it also threatens to substitute certain high-value crops by Northern-based industrial processes.

Many tropical plants cannot be grown in the temperate climates of the North. But their cells — producing the valuable products — could be grown in a laboratory anywhere in the world. Under threat, for example, are the production of insecticides (pyrethrins) from the white daisy-like pyrethrum flowers grown in Kenya, Tanzania and Ecuador, and the production of anti-cancer drugs from the Madagascar rosy periwinkle.

If plant tissue culture is developed to its logical extreme, many of the Third World's "cash crops", such as coffee or cacoa, *could* be produced in factories in London or Boston.

At its simplest, tissue culture is just an efficient — and disease-free — way of taking a multitude of cuttings from a single useful plant. This could be one that happens to produce a high agricultural yield, or that has proved resistant to disease. But it is also the essential basis of plant genetic engineering, which begins by inserting genes into single cells in tissue culture. But it has many variants and many applications.

Tissue and cell culture

In *tissue culture*, a small piece of organised tissue — essentially a mini-cutting — is grown on *solid growth medium*. This is a sterile soil substitute, or a nutrient jelly, which also contains plant hormones needed for plant cells to grow and divide. The cells multiply, and the pieces of tissue can be repeatedly divided until enough has been produced [1].

Tissue or cells for culture can be taken from almost any part of the

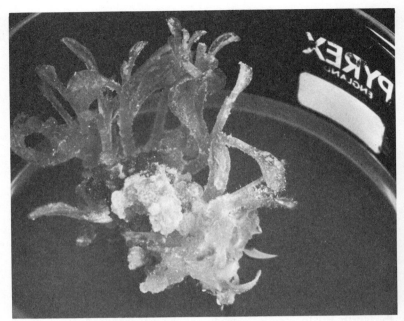

plant (for example, leaf, stem, anther, ovary or seed embryo). Some species prove easier to culture and regenerate than others, and different species are easier with different tissues. The culture of *anthers* (the pollen-bearing tissues) in particular has several advantages (see below) and is widely used in the tissue culture of rice. Already-formed buds can also be cultured and induced to regenerate a new plant — a useful technique for cloning some woody plants such as bananas and plantains (*Musa* species).

The common usage of the term "tissue culture" also embraces an important technical variant — *cell culture*.

In cell culture, plant cells are separated and multiplied in a flask of liquid nutrient. When the flask is full of new cells, single cells or clumps of cells may be picked out and placed on solid growth medium just as in tissue culture.

With the right hormones in the medium, each cell multiplies indefinitely to produce a formless clump — a *callus*. Callus cells are similar to the disorganised masses of cells often produced around wounds or in diseased plants.

Eventually, if treated with further hormones, each tiny piece of tissue or callus can be persuaded to *regenerate*, to produce many tiny "plantlets" — theoretically one from each cell. This process is known as *regeneration*.

Malaysia to clone rattan

In Malaysia, the rattan vine is in the front line for biotechnological development.

Rattan is a climbing palm used by furniture manufacturers in the Philippines and Taiwan to make furniture and partitions, particularly for the Japanese market. It is harvested wild from Malaysian forests.

Rattan is ideally suited to contract farming by local smallholders – lending itself to the sort of smallholder development that has been seen in Malaysia's oil palm and rubber industries.

But prices of US$3,000 per tonne have led to a massive harvesting of the rattan from the forest – causing shortages and thus higher prices. There is even a shortage of planting material for the limited new acreages being planned. Malaysia is therefore researching ways of increasing production. But as tropical forests are felled for their timber, wild rattan vines are felled too.

The only way to boost production seems to be to increase artificially the density of rattan in existing forests, or, as the Forest Research Institute of Malaysia has proposed, to intercrop rattan in rubber or oil palm plantations. As Malaysia does not have enough material for planting, it is turning to tissue culture to produce more plants.

The problem is to establish a complete tissue culture and regeneration process for rattan, as each species of plant needs slightly different procedures, which have to be discovered by trial and error. Practical results may still be two years or more away.

Another task will be to reduce the long period before a new plant sets seed, in order to accelerate crossbreeding.

There is a large gene pool of rattan varieties in South-East Asia (480 out of a recorded 600 world-wide), 104 of which are found in Peninsular Malaysia. At present, only 20 are being used commercially.

Recognising the importance of this multidisciplinary science to the country, the Ministry of Science, Technology and Environment has proposed the creation of a Malaysian Institute of Biotechnology under the next five-year development plan, in order to provide direction and co-ordinate research. Synchronisation with the country's development plans remains essential if Malaysia is to reap the harvest promised by biotechnology.

The trouble with cereals

Crop plants divide into two main classes as far as tissue culture is concerned. One group includes the grasses and grass-like plants, such as cereals, which are all *monocotyledons* or "monocots". They tend to have long narrow leaves, have only one seed leaf on the seedling plant, and grow from the base. As well as the cereals, the monocots also include bulbs, orchids, palms, bananas and plantains, and yams.

The second group comprises the *dicotyledons* or "dicots". These tend to have broad flat leaves, have two seed leaves on the seedling plant and grow from the tips of the shoots and roots. Most vegetables (such as tobacco, potato and tomato — the tissue culture and genetic engineering stars) are dicots, as are most broad-leaved trees.

Unfortunately, monocots as a class, and the cereal grasses in particular, have proved difficult to grow in tissue culture. And since

Making baskets in te Philippines: cloning rattan palm could increase rural incomes in South-East Asia.
/Sean Sprague/Panos Pictures

they include many important staple food crops (for example, rice, wheat, sorghum, millet and maize) this has delayed the wide application of biotechnology to agriculture.

Tissue culture is progressing well, however, in one important cereal — rice. Anther culture has proved quite successful, and rice plants have also been raised from *protoplasts*. These are plant cells which have been gently stripped of their tough cell wall. The protoplast is a particularly useful type of plant cell as without its cell wall it is more accessible to genetic manipulation (see Chapter four). The regeneration of maize plants from protoplasts has also recently been announced, in principle opening up that important crop to genetic engineering [2].

But in all cases, practical results depend on the ease and efficiency of such processes. Success in a few laboratory experiments is not enough. However, there seems to be no fundamental obstacle that will prevent the tissue culture of any plant — given sufficient time and research funding.

In dicots, the source tissue for tissue culture is usually a *meristem* — the very tip of a shoot or root. The meristem is a hemispherical mass of a few hundred rapidly dividing cells. Shoot meristems give rise to the stem, leaves and flowers. Monocots grow from the base (which is why grass can be mown), and do not have localised meristem tissue.

Not all dicots are easy to culture. Woody plants like trees are particularly difficult. And the reasons for this are by no means well-understood, so tissue culture is in many ways more of an art than a science.

'Going fishing'

Developing a tissue culture system for any plant and getting the plant to regenerate in culture can take a long time. An outstanding problem for many species is to find the precise timing of physical and hormonal stimuli that will induce regeneration. In the case of oil palm, it took 15 years to get a working system. And, even then, the experimental system had to be taken back to the drawing board, because after mass production the "cloned" palms failed to fruit.

One plant scientist describes the search for techniques for the successful tissue culture and regeneration of a given plant as "fishing" [3], and another says "recipes, rather than biological laws, have been worked out" [4]. Nevertheless, research is accelerating, and most experts feel that tissue culture innovations will be available within a few years for all plants from grasses to trees. The rate of success will be a combination of luck and research effort, with the latter tending to be greatest for the crops where the money is — the crops of the rich North.

Micropropagation from tissue culture is considered a practical possibility for the following plants, now or in the near future [5]:

Vegetables	Trees and shrubs	Ornamentals
Artichoke	Agave	Carnation
Asparagus	Almond	Chrysanthemum
Beet	Apple	Dahlia
Cassava	Bamboo	Gerbera
Garlic	Banana	Iris
Ginger	Citrus	Lily
Potato	Coconut	Nephrolepis
Raspberry	Cherry	Orchids
Strawberry	Elm	Pelargonium
Sugar-cane	Eucalyptus	Rhododendron
Sweet potato	Ficus (fig)	Rose
Taro	Kiwi	Saintpaulia
Tobacco	Oil palm	(African violet)
	Tomato	Papaya
	Peach	
	Pear	
	Pineapple	
	Plantain	
	Tea	
	Vine	
	Walnut	

Regeneration in the laboratory is now also possible for:

Carrot	Cocoa
Endive	Coffee
Oilseed rape	Jojoba
Maize	Rubber
Rice	Date palm
Soybean &	Hazelnut
other legumes	
Yam	

Producing genetically identical plants by regeneration from cell or tissue culture is known as *cloning* or *micropropagation*.

Some biotechnologists have estimated that, with the tissue culture cloning of selected high-yielding plants, current yields per hectare of oil palm (for palm oil) and castor bean (for castor oil), of tropical trees and bamboo, and of cassava, could be multiplied four to five times. Sugar-cane and groundnut yields could, it is claimed, be doubled or tripled by tissue culture cloning [6].

Mangosteen — described as the most delicious fruit of the tropics [7] — is another example of a tropical plant that could benefit from tissue culture. More trees are needed to meet market demand for the fruit. But each fruit produces only two seeds, and relatively few germinate and produce viable saplings. The present cycle from seed to production takes 8-10 years, so it is extremely difficult to raise production levels. In Malaysia, however, research is under way to produce many new trees from tissue culture, particularly by enhancing the growth of buds in culture. If this research is successful, plantations could be rapidly multiplied and market demand more quickly met.

Tissue culture is also used to multiply orchids — an important cash crop in Thailand — avoiding the need to take large quantities from the wild. Similarly, Malaysia has plans to clone the climbing palm rattan; and Vietnamese farmers have had great success with cloning disease-free potato.

Micropropagation avoids the inevitable reshuffling and separation of genes that occurs in the creation of seed, and ensures that all the offspring are identical. But it means that all the resulting plants are not only as strong as the original, but are also as weak. If a disease arises that can kill the original, it will also kill all the plants cloned from it.

Vietnam's success with potato

In one rural valley near North Vietnam's capital, Hanoi, the tissue culture of virus-free, high-yield potatoes has become a cottage industry, producing millions of plants for the region's farmers more cheaply than imported seed potatos.

The Vietnamese used to grow European potatoes. But imports of new seed tubers fell during the last Vietnam war, and existing stock became infected. The government got scientists working on tissue culture and regeneration. The result: a farmer-friendly technology usable in basic conditions, and not even needing electricity. The equipment is sterilised in home-made autoclaves (high-pressure steamers) made from old US gas cylinders perched on wood fires, and the plantlets are rooted in small banana-leaf pots.

Women, children and grandparents soon became cloning experts. Using a growth medium made from fertiliser solidified with gelatin, each family was able to produce up to 150,000 plants per year. Production in the valley reached 3 million plants at one stage.

John Dodds, of the]International Centre for Potato Research (CIP) in Lima, Peru, visited the project, and was impressed. But he found that the tissue culture material was not completely disease-free and the varieties being cloned were not well-adapted to the locality. So CIP sent in 10 varieties, some with disease resistance, for small-scale trials. The most appropriate were quickly adopted.

In the developing world, potatoes are only the 11th crop in food terms, but in money terms they are already the fourth largest crop after rice, wheat and maize, says Dodds. The potato produces more calories per hectare per year in the form of food than any other crop; and for rural people it is becoming an income-boosting crop, based on the growing urban fast food market. Production has tripled since the 1950s.

Disease-free stock

Many plant diseases and pests are virtually impossible to get rid of once infection has occurred, with the disease being carried through seeds, cuttings or offsets into the next generation of plants as well. One answer is to replant with disease-free, "clean" stock, obtained through tissue culture.

Meristems, used as the source tissue in the tissue culture of dicots, are the only parts of the plant that remain free of virus, bacteria or fungi when the rest of the plant is diseased, so meristem culture is generally clean [8].

In this way, disease-free plant material can also be produced in large amounts. Given regeneration, this allows the multiplication of disease-free plants, and the movement of plant breeding material about the world without fear of introducing disease.

In tropical conditions, problems can arise in maintaining disease-free stocks of tissue or plants. In some cases, virus-free clones have become even more severely affected than before. This is because certain relatively harmless virus infections that inhibit the action of other, more dangerous ones, have been eliminated. Disease-free stock can also only be used to advantage where there is a well-organised distribution and disease-control infrastructure.

Tissue free of various common virus diseases can now be cultured from around 50 types of plants of interest to developing countries [9].

Anther culture for fast plant breeding

Pollen cells from anthers are difficult to culture but offer a special prize to plant breeders in that they contain only one set of genes (they are "haploid"). Plants derived by ordinary pollination have two sets, one from each parent (they are "diploid"). The two sets often carry different variants of any given gene and the two members of this gene pair interact with each other to influence the appearance and physiology of the plant.

Plant breeders are often aiming to produce a line of true-breeding plants with a certain set of desired genes. To achieve this, the plant must have identical copies of the desired gene in both its gene sets, and this can take many cycles of breeding. A quicker way is to double up artificially the gene set of haploid cells in culture and regenerate them into plants.

Haploid cells, or haploid plants grown from them, are also useful in determining what genes are really present in the plant. Many genes are masked by the action of a "dominant" partner in their gene pair in the diploid state, whereas in the haploid state, characters that often remain hidden for generations in a breeding programme can quickly be identified.

For example, with the recent successful anther culture of rice in China, the time from culture to initial yield trials of a new variety is informally estimated to be 18-24 months, compared with three to six years by conventional breeding. However, with rice anther culture the efficiency of regeneration is still low.

Somaclonal variation

Tissue culture can allow breeders to throw a million dice at once.

Somaclonal variation is the natural tendency of cells in tissue culture to alter their genetic constitution. It can provide on the one hand a source of useful variation, but on the other is a hindrance to the maintenance of characters in a clone. The good aspect is that if variation is present, a genetic mixture of millions of cells in a single flask can be subjected in tissue culture to simple stresses such as salinification or high aluminium, to mimic difficult soil conditions. This selects those cells that are genetically resistant to stress and that can be multiplied to produce stress-tolerant plants.

To screen the same number of plants in the field would require a lot of space, a full growing season and substantial labour. Alfalfa, tobacco and rice plants with tolerance to heavy metals, salt and disease have been selected in tissue culture, though research is at an early stage [10].

Stresses that depend on characters of the whole plant, such as drought tolerance (a matter of low water usage and transpiration rates) or wind resistance, cannot be so easily selected in this way.

One of the world's largest experiments in somaclonal variation for developing country crops has been underway for around a decade in the United States at Colorado State University's Tissue Culture for Crops Project (TCCP) [11]. There, Dr Dan Miller, in charge of whole plant testing, said late in 1989 that the greatest practical successes so far had been in sorghum, rice and spring wheat.

The TCCP has produced four lines of sorghum which are resistant to acid soils (down to pH 4.3). These were, surprisingly, selected by stressing cell cultures with high salt and aluminium chloride levels. These sorghum lines should result in a useful product in "two to three years" [12]. Two other somaclonal sorghum variants were by chance exposed to an epidemic of army worm in Georgia, and proved resistant. As army worm is a serious pest in Africa, the TCCP also aims to release these lines.

In rice, TCCP now has several salt-tolerant lines undergoing trials on salt flats in the Philippines, and lines tolerant of highly alkaline soil are under trial in Pakistan. In spring wheat, promising lines are being tested for salt and acid tolerance in Mexico.

A FEW BASICS... plant cells

● In a plant or animal cell, different parts of the cell are specialised to carry out different functions. These subcellular structures are called organelles.

● The most important organelle from a genetic point of view is the nucleus. This contains the DNA, the information store of the cell, contained within a number of separate chromosomes.

● All the living matter outside the nucleus is the cytoplasm. It is compartmented by membranes into several typical organelles, such as the mitochondria – where chemical energy is generated from the products of food breakdown – and chloroplasts (in green plants and algae) – where sunlight is converted into chemical energy by photosynthesis.

● Mitochondria and chloroplasts contain a few genes of their own. Some of these genes are of great interest to genetic engineers as they include genes for herbicide-resistance, and genes for manufacturing enzymes and other proteins involved in photosynthesis.

● The cells of plants, fungi, algae and bacteria, but not those of animals and of protozoa (such as the malaria parasite), are surrounded by a rigid, non-living cell wall. In plants, this cell wall is composed largely of cellulose.

Wide crossing

Protoplasts are plant cells stripped of their tough cellulose wall. The fusion of protoplasts from different plants, to create one cell with two sets of genes, is one way of shifting the most useful genes of tough, wild species (which are usually hardy and resistant to disease) into more delicate — but more productive — cultivated varieties.

Different species of plant, such as rice, Oryza, and its wild relative, Porteresia, will not interbreed with each other naturally, or if they do, will usually produce only a few, poor-quality or aborted seeds.

But protoplasts of two different species have no such barriers. Certain chemical treatments will make two such protoplasts fuse into a single cell containing all the chromosomes (that is, all the genes) of both parents. Plant cells themselves are prevented from fusing because of the presence of the thick cellulose cell wall.

The "hybrid" protoplast is rather an unnatural cell, and as it regrows its cell wall and starts to divide, it usually loses some of the "extra" chromosomes until a genetically stable cell is attained. The resulting cell, and the plant that can sometimes be raised from it, contains a mixture of chromosomes from the two parent species. With a little luck, the "alien" chromosomes that remain will carry the required gene (or genes).

This plant can then be used as a parent in crosses back to the crop parent, which will eventually lead to the introduction of the desirable genes from the alien parent and elimination of any undesirable ones that have been carrried over as well.

In the North, protoplast fusion has already produced new lines of tomato, potato and brassicas [13].

The number of tropical plants which can be regenerated from protoplasts is increasing steadily, as Third World laboratories take up the challenge. Recent success in regeneration from protoplasts in maize, panicum millets, rice, and tropical forest legumes could open a dramatic expansion in breeding possibilities through protoplast fusion.

Variations on the basic technique are also in use. For example, the nucleus of one cell can be extracted and replaced with the nucleus of another. This produces a plant which combines the nuclear genes of one species with genes residing in the mitochondria and chloroplasts of another. Several very useful genes are found in these subcellular structures.

Towards a salt-tolerant rice

Robert Finch at Nottingham University in the United Kingdom, in work for the Rockefeller Foundation rice biotechnology programme, is attempting to introduce salt tolerance into rice. Finch has been using protoplast fusion in an attempt to cross the highly salt-tolerant *Porteresia coarctata*, a wild relative of rice that grows in the sea-shore mangrove swamps of Bangladesh, into a rice species which is relatively easy to regenerate from protoplasts. Porteresia has special "salt hairs" on its leaves, in which the salt is accumulated. The hairs burst, and the salt drops back into the surrounding water.

"The long-term aim of the fusion is to produce a good quality food rice with Porteresia leaves," says Finch. Porteresia and food rice will not interbreed, so protoplast fusion is necessary.

"We want to transfer the whole genome [that is, all the genes] of Porteresia into rice, and then let plant breeders reduce the quantity of Porteresia genes present until we are left with the leaf genes," Finch explains. He recently succeeded in fusing the protoplasts, and has "got the hybrid cells to start dividing".

Embryo rescue

Another method for making interspecies or "wide" crosses is embryo rescue. The cross is made by ordinary pollination, but the resulting embryo would normally abort. Now it can be "rescued" from the ovary before abortion, and grown in tissue culture to produce a viable hybrid plant with an unusual combination of genes.

Dramatic improvements have been obtained in tropical forage legumes, rice and maize through wide crosses made possible by embryo rescue. Several useful species of Phaseolus (field beans) have been generated containing a "wild" gene for the protein arcelin, which confers resistance to several insects [14].

Artificial seeds

Plants formed from tissue cultures are often not tough enough to establish themselves in the field. This makes mass propagation difficult. For some plants, such as potato and yam, the job is made easy by inducing the culture to make miniature tubers, corms and bulbils. In other plants, tiny embryos created in tissue culture — which in normal propagation would be encapsulated in a tough, nutritive coat — can be embedded in desiccating gels for direct planting as artificial seeds. So far, this technique has been applied successfully to greenhouse plantings of carrot and alfalfa [15].

Some agrochemical companies plan to produce artificial seeds containing an embryo engineered for resistance to one of their herbicides (or fungicides), wrapped in a coating of the chemical, thereby selling two interdependent technologies at once.

Phytochemicals: the danger of substitution

Phytochemicals are useful chemicals produced in plant tissue. The chemical reactions needed to manufacture these substances are often too complex to reproduce in the laboratory or in industry, so the plant itself must be the chemical factory.

Two outstanding examples are the alkaloid drugs, vinblastine and vincristine: these are excellent cancer treatments extracted from the Madagascar rosy periwinkle plant which have revolutionised the outlook for children with leukaemia.

Biotechnology is now trying to culture rosy periwinkle cells. The idea is to attempt to replace variable supplies from agriculture in a developing country with industrial production, perhaps in a Northern country. So far, this has not proved entirely successful. The cultured cells do not make enough drug to be useful.

There is no doubt that success in the tissue culture of plant products in the North could be a threat to developing country livelihoods. On the other hand, if it could be adopted by developing countries themselves, it could be a source of income. Much of the immediate impact of biotechnology could depend on how the balance of tissue culture research falls between North and South.

At present, plants are needed to make a vast array of special industrial oils, resins, tannins, saponins, rubber, gums, waxes, dyes, pharmaceuticals and other chemicals. Moreover, most spices, condiments, tea, coffee and cocoa depend on special aromatic and flavoursome chemicals produced by plants. All could be affected by tissue culture substitution [16].

Consider, for example, shikonin, a dye, ointment and cosmetic extracted from the root of a wild herb once collected in Japan, Korea and China, and used to make the red dye of the Japanese flag. Shikonin is now produced in tissue culture in Japanese factories. After much research, cell cultures were developed that contained 20% shikonin after eight months' culture — whereas the plants are collected wild, take four years to grow and produce only 1.4% shikonin. Traditional collectors were thus put out of a job [17].

There have also been fears that far larger numbers of cacao producers could be put out of business by tissue culture. But this is unlikely to occur for the time being as the technology is proving difficult (see Chapter 5).

Bananas and plantains

Bananas and plantains, a group of related palms of the genus Musa, are the most grown fruit crops in the world. They come in many varieties, and are grown around the home to provide shade and a source of carbohydrate. They are cooked and eaten in dozens of ways: for example, the traditional Ethiopian plantain is grown not for the fruit but for the stem, which is ground up, and fermented for several years in shallow pits in the ground for eating later. Many village plantains are cooked, unpeeled, as vegetables [26].

Bananas produce few viable seeds, and are usually propagated by cuttings. Conventional breeding is therefore difficult, and has not led to a single new widely disseminated variety [27]. There is little research on Musa, partly because only 10% of production enters the international cash market. Banana tissue culture of some varieties has been developed through the global research network (INIBAP), managed from Montpellier in France.

A full tissue culture/regeneration/gene transfer system has yet to be developed, but there is progress with the regeneration of banana plants from protoplasts, "and routine regeneration systems will soon be established" [28].

Genetic variation (somaclonal variation) occurring in tissue culture is causing some trouble, leading to plants of different heights and bunch shapes [29].

Some species can now be micropropagated from single buds in tissue culture, and growers can therefore be supplied with plants free of nematodes (root-eating eelworms). Nematode-free stock is already used for establishing new plantations, and for replanting old nematode-infected ones, as the uninfected plants last several seasons before reinfection [30].

Major losses are caused by several diseases, such as bunchy top virus in Asia and some of Africa, the fungal leaf disease black sigatoka, which is spreading rapidly in Africa and Latin America, and fusarium wilt, a soil fungus. Cucumber mosaic virus is also a problem.

Cutting bananas in Dominica. /*Philip Wolmuth/Panos Pictures*

There is big money in phytochemicals. From 1959 to 1980, a quarter of all prescriptions in the United States were for plant-derived drugs. This represented a market of some US$20 billion annually in 1980. The ubiquitous aspirin, for example, although now produced industrially, was originally based on a chemical extracted from the willow tree [18].

Cane-crushing in Bangladesh. A biotechnology sugar substitute has pushed down cane prices.
/Cooper and Hammond/Panos Pictures

The low volume of production of phytochemicals in a plant helps to push up their price — the most dramatic example being the illegally traded psychotropic drugs like cocaine and opium. But even simple rose oil is valued at up to US$5,000 per kilogram, while the Madagascar periwinkle alkaloids are worth $20,000 per gram (US$20 million per kilogram) at retail prices. Clearly, phytochemicals can be big business.

Phytochemicals are often the plant's communications and defence systems: they attract pollinators; they act as pesticides (like the pyrethrins extracted from pyrethrum flowers), allelo-chemicals (which halt the growth of harmful soil micro-organisms or the roots or seeds of competing plants), and plant growth regulators.

Phytochemicals are often made in specialised tissues such as the roots — so any attempt to substitute the whole plant by tissue culture will probably have to reproduce the conditions of those tissues. Already, scientists have developed methods of culturing roots alone, without any green parts, in a system called hairy root culture. Such cultures, which are a kind of "root cancer", may be useful in producing root-derived plant chemicals.

To produce such chemicals in larger amounts from tissue culture, one must be able to:

- Select a high-yielding plant.

- Develop a cell culture technique for the plant's cells.

- Select the highest yielding cells, or an appropriate tissue culture (such as "hairy root" culture).

- Find culture conditions for economically viable production.

So far, relatively little has been achieved along these lines since the last step in particular is proving difficult. But as the biochemical understanding of plant cells improves, more and more substitutions of industrial for plant production will certainly occur.

Meanwhile, there is much to explore in developing countries' under-exploited and uncommercialised plants and other organisms, particularly in the species-rich tropical forests. It is estimated that only 5-15% of the up to 250,000 species of living higher plants have been systematically explored for useful chemicals [19].

Indigenous peoples, in forest areas in particular, have extremely valuable knowledge of the applications of rare plants and trees. They should have a market in selling their knowledge, to help protect their forests.

ENZYME TECHNOLOGY

Enzyme technology is not tissue culture, but is related to it in so far as it can lead to the "industrialisation" of biological processes.

It involves making use of the properties of enzymes, the real worker proteins of the cell. Enzymes are the vital catalysts that direct all the biochemical reactions inside a cell. They can be extracted from any organism, and used to accelerate chemical reactions in industrial processes. The enzymes can be fixed to some porous material with the chemicals to be reacted washed around them, or are sometimes simply mixed with the reactant chemicals in a vat.

It was enzyme technology which enabled US companies to make "high-fructose syrup" from surplus maize, and displace many developing country sugar-cane workers. It can thus be a threat to development [20].

But it could equally be a benefit, if enzyme technologies could be developed to, say, add

Sugar-cane is the main crop on Negros Island in the Philippines. A biotechnology sugar substitute — high-fructose syrup, produced by enzymes from US maize — has lowered cane prices and devastated a once-thriving economy on the island. /*Ron Giling/Panos Pictures*

value to existing biological products, be they cash or food, or to untapped genetic resources in the South. The main problem: enzymatic reactions are generally complex, and require much research to develop and apply.

FOCUS ON PALM OIL

A cautionary tale: the oil palm experience

Individual trees vary greatly in their productivity. Oil palms are no exception. Some may regularly produce triple the oil of their neighbours. Cloning such a tree through tissue culture could triple oil yields.

However, in the Unilever company's efforts to do just this, to improve the productivity of their oil palm plantations in Malaysia and elsewhere, there have been technical setbacks. Their "elite" high-productive clones have flowered badly, and researchers have gone back to the laboratory to work out why. It seems that the tissue culture systems are too unpredictable, and are introducing unexpected changes in the resulting plants [23].

Hereward Corley directs the Unilever company's oil palm cloning project — the world's largest — in Bedford, UK. He explains that the first trial plantations, in 1985, of 40 clones of high-yielding plants over 50 hectares had been very successful. But when the tissue culture system was scaled-up and speeded for mass production (cutting the number of different growth media and corresponding delicate tissue transfers from six to three), the female flowers of the resulting regenerated plants were abnormal and did not develop into fruit.

And without fruit, there is no oil.

Thus the Unilever programme was set back "four to six years". It aimed to increase palm oil productivity from a Malaysian average of 3.5 tonnes of oil per hectare per year to around 5 tonnes. This was an increase of over 40%, and was a conservative goal, given that some clones yield as much as 10 tonnes per hectare per year.

Other plant scientists were amazed that Unilever risked changing the culture regime at all, given the present scientific uncertainties about what is actually going on in tissue culture. A member of the Oxford Forestry Institute, Britain's leading public forestry research body, who blamed over-enthusiasm and commercial greed, felt that the failure was avoidable, and that it had unneccessarily "given tissue culture a bad name".

The flowering abnormalities appear not to be inherited (that is, not caused by genetic changes), but to be due to some disturbance in development.

However, the programme may yet succeed. Unilever has planted out another 70-80 clones, with variations in the tissue culture techniques, in trial production in the nursery.

First fruits of the test are expected in 1991-92. By 1996, Corley hopes, it will be possible to select reliable high-yielding clones for production. "Unilever are taking a long-term view of this," said Corley, and are "still at the beginning" of what can be done.

If the oil palm clone finally proves a success, a possible market of a million seedlings a year will open up in the late 1990s and a major impact on the vegetable oils market will follow. Some 100 million plants would be needed if all the world's plantations were to be substituted with the potentially high-productive, cloned varieties [24].

Palm oil is used as cooking oil; in margarine; as a cocoa-butter substitute; as a fat component in ice-cream; in bakery fat; as a chemical feedstock to produce fatty acids, esters and glycerol, soap, candles, lubricants; as a plasticiser for PVC; in tin plating; and in cosmetics. It is also a rich source of certain dietary chemicals that, it is claimed, may reduce cancer (beta-carotene, tocopherols and tocotrienols mop up "free radicals", highly-reactive molecules which damage DNA and can cause cancer).

Oil palm originated in West Africa, but is now widely grown in Asia and Latin America, with Malaysia the leading exporter of the two kinds of palm oil, one from the flesh of the fruit, and one (high in industrially useful lauric acids) from the kernel.

World production of vegetable oils more than tripled between 1960 and 1984, from 13 to 44 million tonnes a year. Within this total, palm oil quadrupled from 1.5 to 6 million tonnes, 80% of it produced in South-East Asia (60% in Malaysia alone).

The current 25-year life of a plantation is limited by the trees — which fruit at the very top — growing too tall to climb. So one aim of an accelerated breeding programme would be to produce shorter palms. Classical breeding has been slow (as with all trees) as the palms flower only after several years. French plant breeders took 30 years to increase oil palm yields by 35% — and to reduce stem height by 20%.

However, according to L. H. Jones of the University of Cambridge, UK [25], there is at present almost total ignorance of the genetics of yield, quality, drought resistance, wind resistance or disease resistance of the oil palm, of the interaction between the plant and disease organisms, or of the mechanisms of pest resistance. Much basic biology is still to be done, he says.

Not surprisingly, therefore, there are no attempts yet to genetically engineer the palm.

Nevertheless, there is a great opportunity for improvements that could come through breeding programmes speeded up by tissue culture. There is much genetic variation between trees, and many diseases to overcome. Fungus diseases such as fusarium, wilt, and the rot caused by the bracket fungus, Ganoderma, are serious. Pests such as leaf-eating caterpillars, leaf miners and the rhinoceros beetle, also attack oil palm.

To produce plantations resistant to fusarium wilt — a devastating disease — would be a great prize from a cloning programme. It can be tested for at nursery stage. Experimental clones of plants selected in a wilt-resistance programme in Zaire have already been found to be high-yielding as well as resistant, says Corley. It remains to be seen whether they can be easily propagated in a mass-cloning programme.

Another useful goal would be to find and transfer into productive palms the genes for drought tolerance. This would be important in Africa where there are dry seasons of 2-6 months which affect yields. That there are such genes is apparent from certain clear family differences in drought tolerance among oil palms.

CHAPTER 4

PLANT GENETIC ENGINEERING

Tissue culture is a well-established science, with its beginnings back in the 1960s. In contrast, genetic engineering is a newcomer, with the first genetically engineered plant produced only in 1984.

Such is the pace of biotechnology, however, that scientists at the US multinational, Monsanto, which aims to become the "IBM" of genetic engineering, reckon that all major crop species will be amenable to improvement by genetic engineering "within the next few years" [1].

By 1992, it is expected, some 100 useful plant genes will have been isolated and cloned, and 50 or so will have been transferred to other plants which will by then be undergoing field trials. Genetically engineered soybean, cotton, rice, maize, oilseed rape, sugar-beet, tomato and alfalfa are expected to enter the market-place after 1993 — with new genes chosen to suit the largest market: US farmers.

Around 50 important plant genes have been cloned and transferred into other species so far. They include the seed storage protein genes of peas, beans, wheat, maize, and barley, and the tuber storage protein genes of potato; several insect resistance genes; herbicide resistance genes; and the gene for the low-calorie sweetener, thaumatin.

But this is just the tip of the iceberg. A plant may contain around 50,000 genes.

Genes from other organisms, such as bacteria, viruses, and even humans, have also been transferred into plants.

One of the main limitations on the genetic engineering of plants is the availability of so few genes to transfer. According to a leading rice researcher, Professor Edward C. Cocking of the University of Nottingham: "The outstanding challenge is to transfer agronomically useful traits into crop plants using these methods. There are few such traits which are under the control of one or only a few genes and for which genes have been identified."

A FEW BASICS... DNA cloning

● Before a gene can be transferred to another species, it first has to be cloned. The gene is snipped out of the DNA of one organism and transferred into a bacterium. Here it is multiplied up as the bacteria divide, providing a permanent, readily retrievable store of the gene in almost unlimited amounts.

● The total genetic complements of many different organisms are now stored as DNA libraries, consisting of hundreds of thousands of cloned DNA fragments, containing within them all the genes of the organism.

● The molecular biological techniques for cutting and splicing DNA use special enzymes to cut DNA and rejoin two pieces from different sources. This is often called recombinant DNA technology since it involves artificially "recombining" or joining together genes from widely different sources in the test-tube, outside the living cell.

● Before it can be cloned, the gene has to be spliced into a small bacterial carrier DNA (or vector DNA) which allows it to be replicated and maintained in the bacterial cell. The gene plus carrier is known as a recombinant DNA.

● The recombinant DNA can be easily re-isolated from the bacterial culture and then introduced into plant cells in culture as the first step to producing a genetically engineered plant.

MAKING TRANSGENIC PLANTS

A genetically engineered plant must always start with a single genetically engineered plant cell. Genes are introduced into plant cells in tissue culture and these modified cells are then grown up into a plant. This will carry the "foreign" gene in all its cells, and can also pass it on to its offspring in its seeds.

Just 20-30 crops can be genetically "transformed" at present — that is, new genes can be artificially introduced into them to make so-called *transgenic plants.*

The thick cellulose wall of a plant cell presents a real barrier to gene transfer, as DNA cannot penetrate it in order to enter the cell. There are two main ways round this obstacle so far.

Agrobacterium: nature's genetic engineer

The first is to use a natural genetic engineer, the crown-gall bacterium *Agrobacterium tumefaciens* [2]. This bacterium naturally infects a wide range of dicotyledonous plants (many herbs, shrubs and vegetables) but not the grasses and cereals (monocotyledons) such as rice and wheat.   It forms a gall or plant tumour at the site of infection.

Apart from the usual single bacterial chromosome, Agrobacterium contains a small circular DNA — the Ti plasmid. When the bacterium infects a plant, part of this plasmid — the *T-DNA* — is transferred into the plant cell's own chromosomes. The genes carried on the T-DNA force the plant cell to multiply uncontrollably, forming a gall.

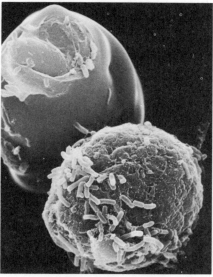

Agrobacterium tumefaciens **bacteria attacking tobacco plant cells, seen through an electron microscope. The bacteria inject parts of their DNA into the tobacco cell. Genetic engineers can insert a desired gene into agrobacterium and so use this natural process to inject the gene into a tocacco plant.** */Dr Jeremy Burgess/John Innes Institute /Science Photo Library*

Any gene introduced into the T-DNA in the laboratory (by routine recombinant DNA techniques) and then reintroduced into the bacterium, is also carried over into the plant's chromosomes and becomes permanently established there. Special Ti plasmids for genetic engineering work have been constructed that lack the tumour-causing genes but can still transfer any inserted gene into plant cells.

Agrobacterium itself is used to infect small pieces of plant tissue in culture. The T-DNA can also be extracted and used on its own as a carrier for transferring genes into protoplasts — plant cells that have had the barrier of the cell wall removed. This is the second chief way of producing a genetically engineered plant.

The drawback of Agrobacterium is that it doesn't infect important crops such as rice, wheat and maize. However, it can be used for some crop plants important to the Third World, such as potato, sweet-potato and cassava, which are all dicots.

The genetic transformation of protoplasts with genetically engineered T-DNA has been successful in a wide range of plants, as the limitation to dicots does not seem to apply at this level. T-DNA has been used to transfer genes into protoplasts of maize, rice and sugar-cane. In the case of rice, plants have been generated from such protoplasts and grown in the greenhouse.

Other techniques

Other techniques for getting genes into plant cells are being developed. The "gene gun" developed at Cornell University in New York State, literally fires genes incorporated into tiny bullets of inert material directly into the nucleus of a cell.

Plant genetic engineering is most advanced in tobacco and tomato, which are easily grown in tissue culture and are natural targets for Agrobacterium.

A FEW BASICS... gene 'expression'

● When a single gene is transferred from one species to another, what is in effect being transferred is the ability to manufacture a particular type of protein.

● For the biological instructions encoded in DNA are instructions for making proteins — the worker molecules of life. Each gene specifies the instructions for the production of a different type of protein.

● Proteins are extraordinarily versatile molecules. They make up most of a cell's structure, and — as enzymes — are essential catalysts for all the life-sustaining chemical reactions that go on continuously inside cells. Many specialised proteins, such as seed storage proteins in plants and antibodies in animals, are also produced for particular purposes.

● Before a gene has any effect it must be "expressed". It must be activated, and start to direct the manufacture of the protein it specifies.

● When a protein is to be made, temporary copies of the activated gene are first made in a slightly different nucleic acid — single-stranded ribonucleic acid (RNA).

● This messenger RNA is then decoded (translated) in a complex biochemical process. Messenger RNA acts as a template for the production of protein chains whose amino acid sub-units are joined together in the order specified by the coded instructions in the gene.

● In genetic parlance, the protein specified by a gene is its gene product, and in directing its production the original gene is said to have been expressed.

In cereals, genetic engineering is currently most advanced in rice.

But even in rice, the efficiency of genetic engineering is very low. Only 1-30 cells in every million treated become genetically transformed. At the University of Nottingham, 10 transformants per million were obtained — "but then we got stuck for 6 to 12 months", say scientists there, trying to regenerate plants from the transformed cells. Eventually a few plantlets were grown. Half were transformed, but in only half of these was the introduced gene active and directing the manufacture of protein.

But it is likely that genetic engineering will get more efficient as scientists learn more about how genes are controlled, and perhaps develop more effective ways of getting genes into plant cells.

So far, genetic engineering in all plants is limited to the transfer of single genes. These are genes encoding useful proteins, such as food storage proteins, or proteins toxic to pests. But many desirable plant characteristics are determined by many different genes working together. Often these are scattered over several different chromosomes, and there is little hope as yet of being able to identify, isolate and transfer them all together. In other cases, however, the genes form a cluster close together on the same chromosome. In these cases, biotechnologists hope to identify useful clusters of genes on the chromosome, and eventually transfer them complete into a target cell.

Techniques such as protoplast fusion (see Chapter 3), rather than single-gene genetic engineering, are at present the only way of making this sort of transfer, and they inevitably bring many other genes along as well.

However, the control and transfer of the numerous genes involved in nitrogen fixation (the conversion of inert atmospheric nitrogen into ammonia, a form which plants can use) from the bacterium-legume association to other plants such as cereals, will take longer than 15 years, a panel of US biotechnologists has predicted [3]. Some researchers even believe that the introduction of the nitrogen-fixing genes from bacteria into a plant could reduce its yield by 20-30%, because nitrogen fixation requires a great deal of energy, which would have to be tapped from the plant's own photosynthetic resources [4].

In the first instance, the commercial exploitation of genetically engineered plants will aim, with the simplest single-gene technologies, at the largest market. This is judged to be that of reducing the costs of Northern farmers in fighting weeds, insects and crop diseases. New tests for diagnosing and detecting disease will also be among the first dividends of this research. Genetic engineers working on developing country crops are likely to have to rely on spin-off from this research.

WEED CONTROL: GENES FOR HERBICIDE RESISTANCE

" Weed control" is the current commercial terminology for using genetic engineering to make crop plants resistant to herbicides, allowing farmers to spray growing crops to kill weeds but not their crops.

An alternative to engineering in herbicide tolerance would be to engineer plants to contain natural weedkillers — for many plants have mechanisms for defending themselves from encroaching neighbours. But little is known about the genetic mechanisms involved.

Meanwhile, Monsanto, which among other agrochemical companies has developed herbicide-tolerance genes [5], claims that its commercial strategy is "to gain market share" for its herbicides, "and not to increase the overall use of herbicides, as popularly held". Sensitive to the fears and criticisms of the environmental movement, Monsanto scientists claim that their research has concentrated on herbicides which need to be applied only in small amounts, have low toxicity, degrade quickly, and stick in the soil rather than washing easily into streams or groundwater.

However, herbicide use may well increase, because farmers will be able to spray them more liberally and often, without fear of damaging their crop. Exactly how much they spray will depend on farm economics, such as the cost of the herbicides and engineered crops, the wages saved through reduced weeding, and the price for which farmers can sell any increased yield.

Monsanto scientists have experimentally engineered genes conferring resistance to the herbicide glyphosate (the active component of the "Roundup" herbicide) into tomato, potato and tobacco. Their present targets: soybean, cotton, corn, oilseed rape and sugar-beet.

Glyphosate kills plants by blocking the action of an enzyme, 5-enolpyruvylshikimate-3-phosphate synthase — EPSPS for short — which synthesises a vital cell chemical. Monsanto is experimenting with three genetic engineering strategies to beat glyphosate:

- Pack the cells of the crop plant with more copies of the gene for EPSPS, so the cell is full of the enzyme. Then the crop will not be affected by the amounts of glyphosate that will be needed to kill weeds.

- Replace the EPSPS gene with a modified one that directs the manufacture of an enzyme resistant to glyphosate.

- Introduce an extra gene whose product will interfere with, and even destroy, the molecules of glyphosate.

Resistance has also been produced in the active ingredients of other herbicides — such as the sulfonyl-urea components of "Glean" and "Oust", and to gluphosinate and bromoxynil. In the latter two cases, the resistance genes come from bacteria that are able to destroy gluphosinate and bromoxynil.

It seems likely that the impact of herbicide-resistant crops will be to reduce the use of weeding labour (an important source of income for landless labourers) on farms that can afford them, and to increase the use of herbicides on such farms. In so far as the system reduces farmers' costs and increases yields, it would decrease the price of the resulting food. This would benefit city dwellers and farmers with a net food deficit, but undercut smaller farmers who could not afford the technology, as happened with the Green Revolution.

This indeed applies to all genetically engineered seeds.

This approach to weed control might prove applicable to cash crops such as cotton, where there is a cash return to pay for the engineered seed and the herbicides. But it hardly seems feasible for rural foods such as sorghum and millet, especially in Africa, where there is little or no market value.

Unprotected worker spraying pesticide on crops near Harare, Zimbabwe. Plants genetically engineered to resist pests could need less spraying.
/Bruce Paton/Panos Pictures

GENES TO KILL INSECTS

Insecticides from bacterial genes

Insect resistance has already been achieved in tomatoes, tobacco and cotton by the transfer of genes from a common soil bacterium (*Bacillus thuringiensis*, or B.t.). The genes direct the production of protein toxins, or poisons, that kill certain insects.

Tomatoes with B.t. gene were completely protected from an attack of caterpillars that stripped other unprotected plants in the same field down to their stalks, scientists reported in a Monsanto experiment [6]. Tobacco has also been successfully protected from the tobacco hornworm with a B.t. gene.

Such plants should offer the farmer many advantages: labour-free insect protection in every season, from seedling to maturity; protection of every part of the plant, even parts difficult to reach with sprays; protection from crop-eating insects without damaging beneficial insects; and confinement of the pesticide to the plant, so leaving soil and groundwater unaffected.

B.t. toxins, which form protein crystals, can also be applied as separate chemicals like any other pesticide, or as whole living bacteria (as described in Chapter 8).

Different B.t. toxin genes are lethal to different insects. So in principle, a B.t. gene can be selected to kill a particular pest, but leave beneficial insects alone. But although many different toxin genes and the corresponding proteins have been isolated, often scientists have no knowledge of what insects they affect. Moreover, many of the B.t. proteins appear to be "glycosylated" — that is, festooned with carbohydrate molecules. Such arrangements are not specified by a single gene, which may complicate the development of an effective B.t. technology.

Although the B.t. proteins are highly toxic to insects, they are claimed to be harmless to people and animals, which digest them like any other protein. Monsanto scientists thus believe there are "early market opportunities" for B.t.-induced resistance in leafy vegetables, potato, maize and cotton. According to some estimates, there is a market of some US$200-300 million waiting for such modified plants [7].

Rice may also be given B.t. protection. Plant Genetic Systems, a private, university-linked biotechnology research company in Ghent, Belgium, with access to some of Europe's leading plant molecular biologists, has linked up with insect scientists at the International Rice Research Institute in Manila. This collaboration aims to transfer B.t. genes into rice to kill rice pests. The target pests are stem-borers (the most damaging group), leaf-folders and case-worms [8].

However, the Ghent scientists say that "there is evidence that insects can evolve around these toxins. So they should only be added to varieties already selected to be resistant by ordinary breeding... The fight against insects will be unending."

Starving insect pests to death

Don Boulter and his colleagues at the University of Durham, UK, have identified a "trypsin inhibitor gene" in an African cowpea supplied by the International Institute of Tropical Agriculture (IITA) at Ibadan, Nigeria. The protein it produces blocks the digestive enzyme trypsin in insects, literally starving them, but is harmless to people. Boulter's group has cloned the gene, and it has now been experimentally engineered into tomato, tobacco and maize [9].

There is a footnote to Boulter's finding: when he later returned to IITA he learned that the original resistant cowpea had been lost from their collections — so he gave them back the gene in a test-tube!

Many other plants have natural insect-killing genes, producing toxins that often give edible plants such as cabbage a bitter taste or smell; in fact, we eat 10,000 times more by weight of natural pesticides than synthetic ones [10]. It seems likely, therefore, that these toxins are relatively harmless to humans, and if identified and extracted could be widely exploited by genetic engineers as substitutes for chemical pesticides.

GENES TO KEEP PLANTS HEALTHY

Scientists in the United States have made tomato, tobacco and potato plants resistant to a broad range of viruses, using a trick that may be useful for many developing country crops, such as cassava. The trick is to "vaccinate" the plant using genes that specify the coat proteins of the viruses that attack them. ("Vaccination" is only a useful figure-of-speech: plants have no immune system as we know it in animals.)

Coat-protein induced virus resistance began with the work of Roger Beachy and colleagues at Washington University, St Louis, and Monsanto scientists. The gene for the coat protein of tobacco mosaic virus (TMV) was transferred into tobacco and tomato. Tomatoes carrying TMV coat protein gene have been tested in greenhouse and field trials and are highly resistant to viral infection. Whereas normal plants suffered losses of 25-70% from tobacco mosaic, the transgenic plants were unaffected.

Protection against alfalfa mosaic virus, potato virus X, cucumber mosaic virus and tobacco rattle virus has been produced by the same technique [11]. There are good prospects for using the coat protein technique for many other plant-virus combinations such as cassava and the African cassava mosaic virus; or rice and the rice tungro virus.

Losses due to African cassava mosaic are large, but difficult to estimate over the whole of Africa: they appear to vary between 4% and 96%, with around 40% for a "resistant" variety. It would be reasonable to hope that full protection could double African yields. Losses from the cassava common mosaic virus reach 30-60% in some areas. An Indian cassava mosaic virus is also serious, and is closely

A FEW BASICS... viruses

● Viruses are submicroscopic packets of nucleic acid (DNA or RNA) enclosed in a protein coat, and can only multiply within a living cell. They are most familiar as the cause of many diseases.

● Once inside a cell, the virus discards its coat and the cell starts copying and translating the exposed viral nucleic acid. Viral genes direct the production of virus coat proteins. So the cell is tricked into making more virus protein coats and more viral nucleic acid. These assemble into new virus particles that are eventually shed from the cell, sometimes destroying it in the process.

● The informational nucleic acid in viruses is either DNA or RNA. Most plant viruses carry RNA, like the well-known tobacco mosaic virus, although a few plant DNA viruses are now known. Animal and human viruses carry either DNA or RNA. Polio-virus, influenza, dengue fever and rabies, for example, are RNA viruses, whereas foot-and-mouth and hepatitis are DNA viruses.

● There are few ways of killing viruses once they have infected a plant or animal. In plants, present control measures concentrate on preventing infection where possible, often by controlling the insects that are instrumental in spreading many viruses from plant to plant.

related to the African mosaic virus [12].

Rice tungro virus is also a "top priority" for control, say the St Louis scientists. "It causes tremendous yield losses — 40-60% in affected fields," they say. It leads to yellow or orange discoloration, stunting, delayed flowering, and the formation of "cancerous" growths in severe cases. The St Louis scientists are working on introducing coat-protein induced resistance into rice. Natural resistance to rice tungro is mostly due to resistance to the plant-hopper insects which transmit the disease from plant to plant. This has been bred into good rice strains, "but it lasts only 4-5 years in the field as the insects adapt", says rice breeder Gurdev Khush of IRRI.

According to Roger Hull of the John Innes Institute in Norwich, UK, the resistance of Green Revolution rice variety IR64 to green leaf-hopper, a vector of rice tungro, has already broken down. The loss of rice from tungro can be estimated at about US$1.5 billion a year, he says. However, rice tungro virus is in fact not one virus, but two: one spherical and the other rod-shaped [13]. The spherical virus is the "transmission agent", helping the viruses to get from plant to plant via its leaf-hopper insect vector; the rod-shaped virus causes the symptoms.

Work at both St Louis and John Innes now aims to transfer the coat-protein gene of one or other of these viruses into rice.

The use of virus-resistant rice varieties in the Philippines could "double or triple production", but new rice technology might find its first applications in industrialised countries, social scientists have warned.

Coat-protein gene resistance is also one of the few strategies available against the bunchy-top virus of bananas and plantains, which causes major losses in Asia and parts of Africa, as no natural source of resistance has yet been found.

A more speculative idea for resisting virus diseases is that of satellite RNA-induced resistance [14]. Some viruses possess separate "satellite" RNAs that seem to reduce the damage done by the virus and slow its spread through the plant. If satellite DNA could be permanently engineered into the plant, it might have the same effect.

DNA copies of satellite RNAs can be transferred into a plant's DNA, where they are translated into RNA. This behaves like natural-satellite RNA, depressing the effects of viral attack. The concept has already been proved experimentally against cauliflower mosaic virus in tobacco.

However, in some conditions, satellite RNA actually increases the virulence of a virus attack, so many scientists counsel against its widespread use until the process is better understood.

HOW LONG WILL SINGLE GENE RESISTANCE LAST?

The resistance produced by genetic engineering to insects and diseases, will, initially at least, be single-gene resistance — because that is all genetic engineering can currently handle.

But traditional plant breeders see big dangers in single-gene resistance [15]. They say, from experience, that pests easily evolve around such single obstacles. So they fear that engineered resistances will not last long. And if resistance breaks down, a new engineered crop would have to be produced. This would only repeat the usual arms race between breeders and plant disease. The resistance of Green Revolution crops has to be constantly maintained by new breeding programmes, for the same reason.

So the key question is: How long can these genes keep the pests at bay?

If the time is too short, the methods will prove uneconomic. Long enough, and they will be practical.

A good breeding rule of thumb has been that the wider the spectrum of pests that a gene or gene cluster resists, the more stable it will be. Coat-protein gene resistance has proved to be quite broad, one type of coat-protein gene protecting against quite a wide range of viruses. But since this is an entirely artificial type of resistance, there is no knowing how it will fare in the real world.

Plant breeders therefore recommend that the genes for several types of resistance against a pest or disease should all be put into the crop at once, to make it more difficult for the pest to evolve around it. But they also doubt that genetic engineers will actually do this, as the more genes transferred, the greater the development time required and the greater the cost.

Some genetic engineers think they can be clever enough to introduce single traits that the virus will find it difficult to evolve around — such as systems that completely block protein production by the virus.

Ultimately, only long testing in the field will tell if these novel resistance mechanisms will be practical and stable.

TESTING FOR PLANT DISEASE

Simple biotechnology-derived tests for disease agents are vital. Promising to be cheap, efficient, and easy to use in the field, they are already available for several diseases [16]. They can be used as tools for tracing the spread of a disease, or for checking the cleanliness of plant materials destined for international transport in breeding work.

However, to be really useful to the farmer, simple diagnostic kits must be accompanied by cheap, effective means to deliver a cure for the disease diagnosed. Such means are rarely available.

Sensitive detection methods use antibodies, which recognise characteristic proteins and carbohydrates on the surfaces of bacteria and viruses, and DNA probes, which recognise the disease agent's nucleic acids.

So-called monoclonal antibodies, in particular, have revolutionised disease diagnosis in plants, animals and humans. They are a highly specific type of antibody, which can be easily mass-produced and virtually made-to-order. Monoclonal antibodies are helping to evaluate disease resistance in plant breeding programmes, to monitor virus-carrying insects such as the brown plant-hopper on rice, and to make rapid on-site diagnoses of diseased crops [17].

DNA probes are similarly selective but latch on to DNA or RNA. They can detect tiny amounts of disease agent DNA or RNA in the plant. They are usually radioactively tagged for detection, which reduces their ease of use or production in developing country conditions. Dye-marked DNA probes are under development, but at present are considerably less sensitive.

Fast and accurate antibody or genetic tests are now available to detect the presence of numerous plant viruses.

GENES FOR HARDINESS: RESISTANCE TO SALT, DROUGHT AND COLD

B reeding for salt-tolerance is likely to be a long and hard task. Some are sceptical of its success. "Salt-tolerant crops will perhaps never compensate for the high concentrations of salt that have accumulated in irrigation schemes through bad management, for instance in Pakistan and part of India," wrote the Asia office director of the Food and Agricultural Organization (FAO) [18].

Resistance to salinity is related to resistance to drought. To the plant, the conditions are similar: both tend to dry the plant out. So research on one problem might help the other.

At the University of Ghent, researchers are seeking genes that are only activated when salt is present. They already claim to have found a protein that appears only in salt-stressed roots. Such a protein is likely to be a protection device of some kind. Powerful molecular techniques now enable scientists to work backwards from the chemical structure of the protein to identify and isolate the gene that encodes it. DNA probes constructed from the gene might then lead

A FEW BASICS... DNA probes

● Extremely sensitive DNA probes can identify the DNA representing a specific gene.

● DNA probes exploit the structure of DNA. DNA molecules are composed of two long chains of chemical sub-units wound around each other to form the famous "double-helix".

● The chemical sub-units of each DNA strand are the "letters" of the genetic message. There are four types of letter (or "base") in DNA — called "A", "C", "G", and "T".

● The two strands of the DNA molecule are held together by pairing between the bases on each strand. A can only pair with T, and G can only pair with C. This is the base-pairing rule which governs all nucleic acid interactions.

● A DNA probe is simply a short length of DNA with a base sequence complementary to a part of one of the strands of the DNA that is being searched for. The probe is synthesised artificially in the laboratory and tagged with some radioactive atom or with a chemical dye that makes it easily detectable.

● When it finds its target it sticks to it by complementary base-pairing, making the target readily identifiable.

● DNA probes are so sensitive that they can detect their target gene in a tiny amount of material — just a drop of blood from a finger, or a small piece of tissue.

to similar genes in other plants, and reveal a constellation of salt-resistance mechanisms.

Virginia Walbot, of Stanford University, is studying the responses of rice to cold which, she claims "is the main environmental factor limiting rice production, affecting the seedlings. One protein that appears [in response to cold] is very like a drought-response protein. And cold stress leads to wilting, just as drought does [19]."

As with salt-tolerance, given the proteins, the corresponding genes may be traced, and the genetic basis of cold-tolerance mapped out. This will aid conventional breeding programmes, as well as offering new genes to transfer between plants by genetic engineering.

GENES TO BLOCK OTHER GENES: ANTISENSE RNA

This exciting new development has been used to most dramatic effect in blocking a gene whose enzyme product — polygalacturanase — causes the ripening and softening of tomatoes. Genetically engineered tomatoes containing antisense genes have been produced that do not go soft on storage, and so have a longer shelf-life [20].

Antisense RNA is thought to work by preventing the translation of its corresponding "sense" RNA — the normal messenger RNA produced by a gene. Antisense RNA is a complementary copy of the sense RNA, and, if the base sequence of the sense RNA is known, a gene that produces the relevant antisense RNA can then be made in the laboratory and engineered into the plant.

This technique could possibly aid in reducing post-harvest losses of some crops: cassava, for example, rots rapidly in storage. However, it would still not prevent pests getting at the stored food.

Antisense RNA could help, however, in eliminating cyanide from cassava. Cyanide is produced by the breakdown of cyanogenic glucosides in the plant. If the genes directing the manufacture of the cyanogenic glucosides could be found, "antisense" RNA could be constructed to cancel their effect. However, these methods would require an understanding — presently lacking — of the genetics, enzymology and significance of cyanogenic glucoside production in cassava. If it were blocked, there might be unexpected negative side-effects, such as increased insect attack.

GENES TO IMPROVE OR CHANGE CROP QUALITY

The quality and value of a crop could be increased by introducing properties that improve the product, for example making it easier to process. Another approach to added value is to produce something completely novel within the plant, treating it as a living chemical factory.

Genetic modification to help food processing and speciality chemical production ultimately "may represent the greatest commercial opportunity", say Charles S. Gasser and Robert T. Fraley of Monsanto [21]. For the food industry, they contemplate modifying cereals, oilseeds and other plants to:

- Produce larger quantities of starches (which are long carbohydrate chains) with various degrees of branching and chain length to improve texture and storage properties of starchy foods.

- Eliminate some fatty acids (supposed causes of heart disease) from seed oils.

- Produce more special oils with particular properties of, for example, viscosity, volatility, temperature sensitivity, mixing properties, etc, for use in food manufacture.

- Produce proteins richer in the essential amino acids.

- Eliminate bad-tasting or harmful components of foods.

- Manipulate colour and flavour.

Coffee plantation in Bali, Indonesia. Coffee is a major developing country crop that could benefit from biotechnology – for example, to make caffeine-free plants.
/Ron Giling/Panos Pictures

Improving food quality

Improving the nutritional value of some cereals is one aim. A rice grain, for example, stores protein in two separate particles, or "bodies", one containing soluble and the other insoluble protein. Only 5-10% of rice protein is soluble prolamine, which the human digestion absorbs easily; 70-80% is insoluble glutelin. The nutritional value of rice could be improved if the useful protein content could be increased.

Professor K. Tanaka, of the University of Kyoto in Japan, is interested in how this distribution between usable and unusable protein is controlled, and how the ratio might be changed and improved.

Many proteins contain signal sequences, which are like addresses and tell the cell where the protein should be sent. In rice, soluble-body signals are different from insoluble-body signals. Tanaka's aim is to construct a gene which combines the code for a high-quality food protein with the code for the relevant signal sequence. The protein would then be directed to one of the protein bodies and useful protein in the grain would be increased [22].

It would also be advantageous to engineer rice to make beta-carotene, from which the body can make vitamin A [23]. Lack of the vitamin means that approximately 5 million people develop xerophthalmia — a thickening of the eyeball — each year, of whom 500,000 eventually go blind. Lack of vitamin A also increases the likelihood of a child dying from measles, diarrhoea or respiratory disease.

But beta-carotene is yellow. Rice producing beta-carotene or some related molecule would also be coloured, which could deter consumers who prefer their rice to be white; often, yellow rice is rejected as old or diseased. Nevertheless, work is in progress to extract the genes for the beta-carotene manufacturing system from blue-green algae, for potential use in rice and other food plants.

Speciality chemicals

There are also "enormous opportunities" for the use of plants for speciality chemicals, Gasser and Fraley believe. Many plant products have been replaced by synthetics made from mineral oil, but in principle the plant sources could be modified and improved by genetic engineering to re-challenge their old markets or find new ones.

Developing countries might be able to use these techniques to improve their traditional and dwindling product sales. However — and it is a big however — this could only happen if the relevant research is done. The costs would be high, and the returns unpredictable.

Plants could also be modified by introducing human genes so that seeds contained medical products such as blood clotting factors or growth hormones. These would not be eaten: the farmer would send them to a chemical company to extract the useful chemical. The

A peasant's maize store in north-west Tanzania: maize has become a key home-grown African food. But if it could be genetically engineered, would it be improved to suit Africa – or the major Northern producer, the USA? /Jan Hammond/Euro Action Acord/Panos

farmer would be using the field as a solar-powered chemical factory.

Already Arabidopsis (a small cress-like plant) has been experimentally engineered to make human enkephalins — brain hormones that affect mood — and tobacco has been engineered to make human antibodies [24].

Rapeseed is also wide open to such alterations. It is already a significant crop in India, Pakistan, Bangladesh and China, and also in Europe and North America. A Canadian variety ("canola-grade") with low levels of compounds that interfere with digestion in the meal, has set the standard for international trade. The molecular understanding of the process by which rape plants make their oils is increasing rapidly, to the point that they could soon be modified by genetic engineering [25].

Biotechnology could move rapeseed ahead of other oil crops in the market, by improving its productivity and the fatty acid composition of its oil. There is increasing demand for speciality oils for food and industrial use, and rapeseed could be engineered to meet this market. It could then displace other special oil sources such as coconut or palm kernel oil, plants for which gene transfer systems do not yet exist.

There may also be new opportunities for flax, easily grown in India and China. Flaxseed produces linseed oil for industrial and craft uses. A significant reduction in the linolenic acid in the oil has produced a flax plant that now makes a food oil of similar quality to sunflower oil. This could help China and India reduce their current huge deficits in food oils.

CHAPTER 5

THREE CROPS: COCOA, CASSAVA AND TREES

B iotechnology will affect many crops, both cash crops and food crops. Three cases illustratè the multitude: cocoa, a cash crop of both plantation owners and small farmers; cassava, the major carbohydrate source of Africa; and trees, used for many purposes from producing fruit to rubber, oils and timber.

COCOA BIOTECHNOLOGY: FOR OR AGAINST THE POOR?

C ocoa, produced from the cacao plant (*Theobroma cacao*) is one of the most important agricultural commodities on the international market. Sales of US$2.6 billion annually place it fifth after sugar, natural rubber, coffee, and cotton.

The key to its saleability is cocoa butter whose very specific qualities of consistency, melting point, and taste are difficult to copy. The fat is hard at room temperature yet melts at body temperature, making cocoa butter useful not only in chocolate production but also for toiletries.

Some 54% of world production comes from Africa, 36% from South America and 10% from Asia and Oceania. Broadly speaking, West African countries such as Côte d'Ivoire, Cameroon, Ghana, Benin and Togo are the least prosperous producers, while Brazil and Malaysia are the most prosperous. This reflects the fact that the bulk of producers in Africa are smallholders growing older varieties, whereas in Malaysia and Brazil some traditionally bred higher-yielding hybrid trees are cultivated, mostly on large plantations.

Three companies currently control world trade in cacao beans: Cadbury-Schweppes, Nestlé (now incorporating Rowntree), and Gill & Duffus. Nine companies dominate chocolate manufacture, which is almost exclusively located in the northern hemisphere: Nestlé, Cadbury-Schweppes, Interfood, Mars, Gracem, General Foods, United Biscuits, Monheim, and Suchard.

Cacao is indigenous to Amazonia. The genetic base of cultivated

Harvesting cacao bean on a plantation in Java, Indonesia.
/Ron Giling/Panos Pictures

cacao is small, being derived from a few plants collected around 50 years ago. This narrow genetic base makes cacao a disease-prone crop which is liable to major fluctuations in yield and quality. Supply and price are therefore unpredictable.

But cacao is easily crossed and bred, and there is a wide degree of genetic variation available — for example, in wild species in the Amazon jungle. But less traditional breeding has been done in cacao than in coffee [1].

Cacao is often cited as the crop most likely to be radically affected as a result of developments in biotechnology — not because of what might be done for the plants in the field, but what might be done to replace them with Northern, factory-based, biosynthetic technologies.

There are several lines of biotechnology research being applied to cacao in the United States, Europe and Japan:

- "Biosynthesis" of cocoa butter in cell culture.

- Genetic engineering of cacao plants to increase fat production.

- Development of "enzyme technology", other oilseeds and processing methods to produce new and better cocoa butter equivalents by conversion of cheap surplus vegetable oils.

- Cloning high-yielding, disease-resistant cacao trees.

Research, funded by the chocolate industry, into tissue culture of high-yielding and disease-resistant cacao varieties could, if successful, lead to over-production. If pursued on plantations, it would push smallholders — and countries whose exports depend on their crop — out of the market.

However, practical and commercial success in this research is proving elusive, and in the short term it is unlikely that developments will impact dramatically on current production patterns. Tissue culture for cacao is not well-advanced: there is no anther culture, liquid culture or protoplast culture for the plant. Immature embryos have been regenerated, but not successfully planted out. So the application of even the simplest biotechnologies to cacao seem far off.

Early predictions that cocoa butter could be produced in tissue culture are therefore no longer taken seriously. It is doubtful that it is even possible, due to the complexity of the cocoa butter production mechanism in the cacao plant (which is itself very poorly understood). Even if it were possible, it would almost certainly be prohibitively expensive — US$200 per tonne compared with $9 per tonne for real cacao.

On the other hand, in 1986, the American Cocoa Research Institute and the Chocolate Manufacturers' Association endowed a tissue culture research programme at Pennsylvania State University for US$1.5 million, with a different aim: to clone good plants, and hence increase production. This is probably the largest single programme on cacao; but there is other publicly and privately funded research work in the United Kingdom, France, Côte d'Ivoire, Ghana and Costa Rica.

Professor Paul Fritz, head of the programme at Pennsylvania State University, claimed in July 1989 to have made "modest progress" in perfecting a method of growing cacao trees from axial buds using tissue culture methods. "Success could come at any time, although I wouldn't like to predict how long it will be before we have a perfect method," he said.

Opinion elsewhere, however, is sceptical. Janet Blake, a specialist in micropropagation at the University of London, says: "It can be done, but no one to my knowledge has been able to find a way to repeatedly clone cacao on a satisfactory scale. A lack of scientific understanding of cacao plant physiology is limiting progress."

Once available, high-yielding disease-resistant cacao clones would quickly be grown on plantations. But in the opinion of the American Cocoa Research Institute, "small growers would be unable to use adequate fertiliser and chemicals" for the elite varieties, which would demand feeding and protection just as did the Green Revolution dwarf wheats and rices.

Limited access to the training and resources required to sustain rapid introduction of new cacao varieties would also hamper small farmers; Africa would thus tend to be pushed out of the market.

Tissue culture techniques are unlikely to be patentable, however.

Despite his funding coming from the chocolate industry, Professor Fritz is adamant: "I am entitled to publish my work and make my results available to all. In the end, small farmers will benefit simply because the advances are being made."

Fritz adds: "When I first went to Ghana to discuss my research on cacao, the first thing my Ghanaian colleagues asked me was whether my work was designed to take something away from cacao-producing countries."

In fact, a stable and effective indigenous research programme, able to monitor, implement and disseminate advances in cacao varieties to small growers, is essential in Africa and elsewhere if the less prosperous cacao-producing nations are to benefit.

Cocoa butter equivalents

To get around fluctuations in cacao supply and price, the edible oils industry has for more than 20 years sought to develop "cocoa butter equivalents" (CBEs).

Unilever now holds half the world market in such equivalents, having bought up Calve, Croklaan, and Loders and Nucoline, three early developers of CBEs. Other companies involved include Fuji, Arhus Olje Fabrik, Karlshamm and Friwessa.

The world market for CBEs has always been limited by their taste — which fails to imitate cocoa perfectly. Nevertheless, that market is currently some 200,000 tonnes, which is equivalent to 500,000 tonnes of cacao beans or a quarter of the world production of cacao.

One approach to CBEs is enzyme engineering. With recent advances in enzyme technology it is now conceivable to use genetically engineered enzymes to convert low-cost vegetable oils into CBEs. But so far, the technique has proved prohibitively expensive, and at the present (low) price of cocoa it is uneconomic.

Nevertheless, American (Genencor) and Japanese (Kao Corp) companies are developing and seeking to patent enzymes that will fractionate vegetable oils into the constituents for CBEs. Research has also developed alternative routes for producing CBEs involving the blending of cheap palm and sunflower oil fractions. Loders and Nucoline, a Unilever subsidiary, currently blend a cheap fraction of illipe (Borneo) and sal (India) oils with shea stearin (Côte d'Ivoire) to make CBEs.

Like cocoa butter, these natural substitute fats all come from wild rather than plantation oil crops. Therefore, like cacao supplies, they are prone to political and seasonal instability. They are also of themselves important export crops for some poor countries. For example, shea represents over 10% of the exports of Burkina Faso.

Having led the development of cloned oil palm, Unilever is also developing a method for making CBEs by blending cheap fractions of potential surplus plantation oil crops such as palm oil and sunflower oil with stearic acid available from oilseed rape.

The market is now glutted with cheap palm and other vegetable oils, generated largely from over-production in the North. Palm oil is the leading constituent of CBEs but whale, fish, olive, soya and sunflower oils are all mentioned as raw materials on Japanese patent applications to the European Patent Office for high-quality CBE enzyme techniques.

The thrust for these developments is coming from the edible oils industry. Chocolate manufacturers have a mixed opinion about CBEs, as typified by Cadbury-Schweppes' insistence that "cocoa butter comes from the cacao bean. No imitation, however equivalent, can ever be legally marketed as cocoa butter under the UK trades, description law." Nevertheless, Cadbury-Schweppes possesses technology to produce CBEs, and the chocolate industry has lobbied equally with the edible oil industry for relaxation of European regulations governing the use of CBEs in "chocolate".

There are also limited indications that these developments are being allied to the genetic engineering of oilseeds by companies such as Calgene in the United States. Genetic engineering of oilseed rape is the most advanced while sunflower and soya are both serious candidates. Tailor-made oilseeds, producing fat of a certain quality, could certainly alter the feasibility and economics of CBE production.

Given the substitution of sugar by artificial sweeteners and the production of high-fructose syrups from maize (an early application of biotechnology), once oil crops in the North become sources of constituents for high quality CBEs, increased protective trade barriers could further exclude cacao-producing countries from the market-place.

'REVOLUTION' POSSIBLE FOR CASSAVA

"There are few crops where science could have as revolutionary an impact as with cassava," claimed US Agency for International Development official R. Bertram in a report to the World Bank in May 1989 [2].

The great target would be to reduce the effects of cassava mosaic virus — an "absolutely devastating" disease in Africa, says Professor G.G. Henshaw, a cassava specialist at the University of Bath, United Kingdom. "If we could reproduce genetically altered, mosaic virus

The roots of cassava –
like this plant in Cape
Verde – provide
Africa with most of its
calories. But the plant
is susceptible to
several pests. / *Ron
Giling/Panos Pictures*

resistant cassava clones it would be a tremendous benefit to African
farmers."

In Africa, cassava has the highest annual tonnage of all food crops
(50 million tonnes) [3]. The world tonnage is 137 million, grown on
14 million hectares.

A hardy tropical shrub with a tuberous root which stores much
starch, cassava is a "safety net" crop for 300 million poor farmers —
particularly in Africa, where it provides 40% of calories consumed,
and to a lesser extent in Thailand, where it is a cash crop grown to
make tapioca, and in Latin America. It has a nearly unmatched degree
of drought tolerance, flexibility in planting dates, and yield [4].

But it has major drawbacks. It takes hours of women's labour to process (in West Africa, women spend nine hours processing five kilograms of cassava into gari, the regional cassava meal dish); if not thoroughly processed, it produces cyanide. It is very low in protein; it suffers from a large variety of pests and diseases; and it deteriorates rapidly — in one to three days — once dug up, unless quickly processed into flour or some other meal. Urban consumers tend to reject it in favour of less difficult foods, so it is primarily a crop for rural areas.

Virus-free meristem culture has removed one barrier to improving cassava — the movement of genetic stock between Africa and Latin America for breeding.

Particularly in Africa and Latin America, there are many varieties of the plant to use in breeding and genetic research. The culture collection at the Centro Internacional de Agricultura Tropical (CIAT) in Colombia, the international agricultural research centre most concerned with cassava, includes 5,000 cultivated forms and 30 wild species [5]. But because of the African cassava mosaic virus, it is too dangerous to import whole plants into Latin America.

Scientists at the International Institute for Tropical Agriculture in Ibadan, Nigeria — the centre for cassava work in Africa — create virus-free meristem tissue from African varieties, and send it to the Scottish Crops Research Institute — where it is tested and certified virus-clean. Once cleared, it goes to Henshaw's group at Bath which multiplies the material and sends it to CIAT.

CIAT can then regenerate the plants it wants. This neatly avoids the inherent risks of transferring live plants and allows researchers access to germplasm that would otherwise not be available.

The regenerated, virus-free stock also yields very well in virus-free research plots. Protected against virus reinfection, yields per plant are initially three to four times more than the normal disease-ridden field varieties. A virus-free clone developed at the University of Zimbabwe has reached 50 tonnes per hectare, compared with the average rural yield of only 2-10 tonnes. Stable yield increases of 70% have been reported. In China, well-adapted micropropagated clones (known as CM 321-188) from CIAT are generating 30-70% yield increases, sustainable thus far, with 30,000 hectares of Chinese farmland due to be planted to the clones in 1989 [6].

However, in African farm conditions, where the viruses are widespread and there is little experience of keeping virus-free crops separate from infected ones, reinfection can occur in months — a much shorter time than the cassava life-cycle, says French cassava researcher Claude Fauquet [7].

The reinfection rate determines how rapidly farmers must be resupplied with fresh clones to maintain the high yield. A high reinfection rate can be lived with if distribution systems are good and costs are kept low. The only place where this happens is Cuba, says Henshaw: "Routine cultivation of virus-free cassava is possible in Cuba because under the state-controlled system distribution of new clones is easy."

Elsewhere, the small farmer would need a strong incentive to spend money on virus-free plants, when all he usually has to do is replant a stem from his old stock. "We have to find a way to make it advantageous to the farmer to replant clean material," says Henshaw. "There are signs that this is happening in India where an Indian biotechnology company offers clean material to farmers and guarantees to buy back the tubers for manufacture of dextrose and sorbitol. This seems a realistic way to introduce virus-free clones."

There is little data available about the reinfection of cassava once reintroduced, says Henshaw, noting: "This basic epidemiological research simply has not been done."

Cassava can now be micropropagated from leaf cuttings. Work is also progressing to establish a full cassava tissue culture cycle, including somaclonal variation, "somatic embryogenesis" (the generation of a true plant embryo from an ordinary piece of plant tissue), regeneration from protoplasts, anther culture and genetic engineering.

Cell cultures of cassava have been genetically transformed with Agrobacterium T-DNA. But so far, leaf cuttings, which can regenerate, cannot be transformed, and single-cell cultures cannot be regenerated, so the two technologies have not yet met to produce genetically engineered plants.

In June 1989, Ian Robertson of the University of Zimbabwe said the university had some genetically transformed plantlets in tissue culture "two inches high with roots", but the work has not yet been recognised elsewhere.

Two international research networks on cassava have recently been established: the Advanced Research Network on Cassava, by CIAT; and another, Cassava-Trans (the "Trans" standing for "transformation"), by the French developing country research agency, ORSTOM, and Washington University, St Louis, Missouri, in the United States.

The founders of Cassava-Trans have been seeking funding "to create cassava that is better adapted to its native environment rather than to develop new technologies" [8]. However, they will need new technologies to meet their goal. In particular, they must develop a gene transfer system for cassava. Ultimately, the network aims to introduce virus-resistance genes into cassava varieties that are popular with farmers, with processors, and with consumers.

According to Claude Fauquet, one of the founders of Cassava-Trans, conventional breeding for virus-resistant cassava can disperse and weaken the traits that make a variety popular; genetic engineering, which can introduce a single virus-resistance gene with surgical precision into the plant genome, can leave these traits unharmed.

Other genes targeted for eventual introduction are ones that would improve the poor protein content of the crop — as has already been attempted with potato — and *Bacillus thuringiensis* genes to kill insect pests.

A collaboration between CIAT and CIP (the International Potato Research Centre in Peru) and Louisiana State University is aiming at introducing the gene for potato storage protein into cassava [9].

The Advanced Research Network on Cassava, established in 1988 with seed money from the International Fund for Agricultural Research, aims to develop a world-wide programme for biotechnology research into cassava [10]. In September 1989, it began to seek funding from bilateral and international agencies. Research targets include reducing cyanide content, improving storage properties, improving starch and protein content, increasing the efficiency of photosynthesis, increasing insect resistance, developing propagation from seed, and introducing virus resistance.

The programme will be modelled on the Rockefeller Foundation's International Rice Biotechnology Programme. It will be aimed at Africa and other areas where cassava is a major food staple.

"There is a significant need for African training programmes and facilities, country by country, to support work on cassava", says Professor Henshaw, who is a member of the steering committee.

BIOTECHNOLOGY TO SAVE THE FORESTS?

Trees are grown in village woodlots for fuel and construction materials; in shelter belts to protect areas from erosion; in agroforestry systems that mix trees with non-woody crops — often to help shelter those crops from excessive sun or wind, or to provide nutrients; in commercial plantations; and otherwise for wood, fruit, gums and saps (as with gum arabic and rubber), oils from leaves, bark, or other special products; and in managed and unmanaged natural forests.

Over half the wood used each year is burned locally for energy, mostly in developing countries for cooking. But on the world market, trade in forest products amounts to US$120 billion, of which US$80 billion is trade with developing countries [11].

Biotechnology will affect many sorts of trees and their uses in one way or another, but in the long term rather than the short.

The "low-tech" cloning of tropical hardwoods, by coppicing (felling the tree, allowing the stump to shoot, and cutting and replanting the shoots) should be "well within the capabilities of rural communities", according to Dr Roger Leakey of the UK Institute for Terrestrial Ecology (ITE) at Penicuik. ITE is working with Nigeria and Cameroon on cloning hardwoods.

Forests of varying degrees of cover grow on around 5 billion hectares, or about one third of the Earth's land surface. However, tropical forest is being lost at the rate of 5-20 million hectares per year. New, or replanted, forests are being introduced at around 14 million hectares a year, of which only 6 million is in the tropics [12].

"There is a pressing need for more extensive and productive plantations — and their establishment and management should incorporate appropriate new technology," says John Burley, director of the Oxford Forestry Institute (OFI), in the UK.

Biotechnology could help by:

- Making clones of old, highly productive trees. Cuttings from mature trees usually do not grow, and whereas those from juvenile trees do, it is very difficult to predict whether a juvenile tree will be highly productive or not, making breeding programmes somewhat hit-and-miss.

- Enhancing the rooting and survival of trees on difficult sites.

- Developing new products, including the bio-digestion of waste wood with microbes.

- Increasing the movement and use of disease-free stock.

Kenya smallholders win out

In tea improvement, Kenyan smallholders have taken the lead over plantation owners, according to a report prepared for the International Labour Office by L.P. Mureithi and B.F. Makau [17].

Kenya is the world's fourth largest tea exporter, producing 11% of the tea on world markets. Two-thirds of the tea is grown by smallholders ("outgrowers"). More than one in ten Kenyan small farmers grow some tea on their farms — and all of the smallholder teas are clones of improved varieties developed by the Kenyan Tea Research Association.

Smallholders adopted these better-selling varieties when they first turned to tea growing a few years ago, the report notes. They did not have the costs faced by the large plantations of replacing their existing stock of plants, and so could adopt the best available — indicating a possible advantage of small-holders over plantation owners when biotechnology brings new varieties of woody, long-lived plants.

Tapping on a rubber plantation in Malaysia: biotechnology could clone more productive trees, to help natural rubber producers attack the growng market for rubber substitutes. /*Trygve Bolstad/Panos Pictures*

• Helping to conserve genetic resources.

Classical breeding is difficult with trees as it requires both space and long periods of time — up to tens of years — for the trees to mature, flower and seed.

After 40 years' work, classical tree-breeding has its successes: for example, the Oxford Forestry Institute has identified strong populations and individual trees of several tropical species, and is now providing breeding populations to developing countries. The cost of the research has been US$8 million; but if countries use the improved material at the current rate of planting unimproved samples, the benefit by the year 2000 is estimated at US$1.5 billion [13].

Biotechnology can help by rapid micropropagation and multiplication of particularly good tree specimens. Culture of virus-free tissue and anther culture for rapid breeding-in of desirable traits would be very useful in reforestation.

Regeneration from anther and pollen culture has been achieved — in the laboratory — for several woody species including *Coffea arabica* and rubber [14].

Biotechnology can also help by surveying the genomes of a population of trees and finding correlations between genes — or gene products — and useful adult characteristics. Then the genes — or products — could be sought in the juvenile trees with molecular techniques.

Cloning work is under way in many countries — including

Australia, Brazil, Canada, Europe, Japan and the United States — on more than 60 tree species. Clones can be made by "micrografting" the meristems of a tree onto rooted seedlings. In Brazil and the Congo, large areas are already being replanted by the rejuvenation of old trees by coppicing. Century-old redwoods and teaks have been successfully cloned.

Plantation owners are already attempting to use tissue culture to clone the "best" fruit trees, oil palm, date palm, coconut palm, cacao trees, ornamental trees, and wood species for timber and pulp.

One paper pulp company — Aracruz, in Brazil — raised pulp output 137% in seven years by propagation of cuttings from selected high-pulp-productive, coppiced eucalyptus.

However, the only forest trees which currently benefit from commercial micropropagation are wild cherry and aspen.

Unfortunately, as with oil palm, the expected advantages of producing an exact genetic copy of the initial tree are often altered by the persistence in the clone of variations — such as abnormal flowering and poor fruits in oil palm — which develop in the tissue culture. The cause of these changes is still a mystery. Quite considerable differences may develop between the expected and actual productive gain from the clone.

Among fruit trees, mango, papaya and clove have been regenerated in Florida with some success. But as with tropical pines, eucalypts and palms, lengthy field trials are needed before it is clear that tissue-cultured trees will be successful. Breeders are targeting growth-rate, shape (to ease fruit picking by reducing stem height, for example), and flowering characteristics [15].

Many billions of hectares of developing country land which are under-productive because of saline, metallified or otherwise poor soils (there are 150 million hectares of wasteland in India alone) could be reclaimed for forestry if species tolerant to these conditions could be selected and cloned. Biotechnology could help select and propagate Acacia, Prosopia and Sesbania tree species, which fix nitrogen, to maintain soil fertility and protect against erosion.

The genetic engineering of trees is less advanced than their cloning. Yet the plant genetic engineers' main tool for transferring genes, the bacterium *Agrobacterium tumefaciens*, has been used to genetically engineer important US timber trees (Loblolly pine and Douglas fir). Resistance to diseases and chemical stresses such as salts and herbicides will be engineered in and selected through tissue culture, and breeding rates will be greatly increased [16].

In the genetic conservation of tree species, cryopreservation of germplasm would also reduce the present need to plant vast areas with trees whose seeds do not store well.

Protoplast fusion has created citrus grafting stock resistant to cold and disease, has reached laboratory-stage regeneration with sequoia, but has not yet succeeded with conifers and eucalyptus.

Another option, apparently peculiar to trees, is to take cuttings from particular parts of a tree, and to preserve the properties of those parts (such as form, and resistance to disease) in the resulting clones.

CHAPTER 6

BIOTECHNOLOGY AND HUMAN HEALTH

CORNUCOPIA OR PANDORA'S BOX?

In the North, medical biotechnology is offering a cornucopia of new developments. These include drugs that are now produced by genetically engineered bacteria (see Chapter 8); faster blood tests using monoclonal antibody or DNA probes; new approaches to mood control through work on brain messenger chemicals; and treatment for infertility through in vitro fertilisation (IVF). Molecular biology is also beginning to reveal the complex path to cancer, one of the remaining major killers in industrialised countries. And there is the promise of gene therapy to correct genetic disease. Plans to read out the complete genetic message encoded in a human being's genes (the human genome sequencing project) also have untold consequences for medicine — and for society.

But most of these glamorous achievements of medical biotechnology are at present of little relevance to most developing countries. In the North, health budgets range from US$500 to US$1,500 per capita per year, according to the World Health Organization. In the poorest countries, however, health budgets hardly reach US$4 per capita per year. In such countries, biotechnology could have a real impact in providing low-cost methods for the prevention and treatment of infectious and parasitic diseases.

When they do arrive in the South, however, some of the more dramatic medical biotechnologies may open a Pandora's box — as they have in the North — raising enormous and unsolved human issues which will be dealt with differently in every culture, be it Muslim, Buddhist, Hindu, Catholic, Protestant, or Animist. Every culture should prepare itself for the shock.

Embryo technology

Many of the questions gather around the techniques that have been developed for fertilising human eggs outside the womb — in vitro fertilisation — and reimplanting them, either in the womb of the genetic mother or in another woman. Coupled with the new DNA

Human gene therapy

Human gene therapy is often touted as one of the potential benefits of the most advanced new medical technologies. It aims to treat those fatal human diseases and genetic disorders for which there is no treatment at present, but which might, in principle, be ameliorated by introducing a compensatory gene into the patient's own body cells.

The introduced gene would, for example, make some product that is lacking, as in the case of many hereditary diseases. Outstanding developing country examples include two blood disorders: thalassemia and sickle-cell anaemia, which are due to faulty genes for components of haemoglobin — the protein that carries oxygen in the blood. An introduced gene might also be effective in preventing the development of a fatal disease such as AIDS or cancer.

Gene therapy would be given to affected patients after birth, or after the disease arises. Initially, plans for human gene therapy centred on correcting bone marrow cells, which give rise to all blood cells. But successfully modifying bone marrow has proved far more difficult to achieve than envisaged, and scientists are now turning to other routes to deliver therapeutic genes.

One possible route is by the implantation of artificial organs or organoids which would be composed of cells making the required product. Progress has been made in experimentally generating organoids in the laboratory, using synthetic "Gor-tex" fibres as a base. Some types of cell will form a tissue around the fibres, and if this ball of tissue is implanted into the body cavity of an experimental animal, blood vessels will begin to grow into it and connect it with the animal's own bloodstream, making a kind of artificial organ [14].

The eventual aim is to make organoids for implantation into human patients, using their own cells which have been genetically modified outside the body so that they are able to produce the required product. This would then continuously feed into the patient's own bloodstream for circulation around the body.

Although scientists are excited about the potential of organoids, any practical benefits to patients are still many years away.

technology of gene detection, transfer or modification, this leads to many possibilities, desirable and undesirable.

Already the possibilities are:

- Children with two mothers — one genetic, who donated the egg, and one who carried the embryo and gave him or her birth.

- Ways of detecting the sex of IVF embryos before reimplantation in the womb. This raises the possibility that parents could choose the sex of their children, and that this choice could be abused to produce an imbalance of one sex.

- Stored frozen fertilised eggs whose genetic parents have died. Such a case occurred recently in Australia, where a judge had to decide what should be done with these potential human beings. There has also been a court case in the US where a separated couple fought over who should have custody of their stored fertilised eggs, and whether the woman could use them to become pregnant without the consent of her former partner.

- The ability to grow a fertilised egg in the laboratory, raising the ethical question of how much, if any, experimentation should be allowed at this stage. Is the fertilised egg to be considered a human being right from the start and all research on it banned? Or alternatively, at what point — how many cells — does this microscopic ball of cells become a human being and research must stop?

Still in the realms of science fiction are:

- Genetically modified human eggs or embryos. Although it is theoretically possible to introduce a gene into a human egg, this has not yet been done, for both technical and ethical reasons. Techniques for transplanting genes into mammalian eggs outside the body and then reimplanting the eggs in the womb are still very inefficient. In the laboratory mouse there is still a high failure rate in raising genetically modified animals. So even if it were considered ethically desirable to correct a genetic defect in humans in this way, the techniques are still far too risky.

- Cloning human beings by separating the cells of a dividing fertilised egg, and growing each up to make a new embryo for implantation.

- Storing clones of an individual's embryonic cells to provide "spare parts" later on to repair the effects of disease or injury, or even to grow an identical twin after an individual dies.

The human genome project

Other concerns have arisen along with plans to map and read out the human genetic message (the human genome) in its entirety, which could have many medical benefits in identifying genes involved in disease. Read-out (technically called DNA or gene sequencing) will be costly and will be done partly under private and partly under government sponsorship. Private companies will certainly claim "ownership" of the sequences they find, demanding royalties for their use. The US Congress is already considering a proposal from the co-discoverer of the structure of DNA, James Watson, that parts sequenced under US national funds should remain US property, if other countries do not help fund the sequencing programme. Watson's remarks were particularly directed against Japan, but they apply with equal force to developing countries which will not be able to afford to be part of the multimillion-dollar sequencing programme.

Related to that are concerns about the gene probing of individuals, which will be possible when the human gene map is complete, to

A FEW BASICS... DNA sequencing

● The DNA molecules in human chromosomes are each made up of millions of chemical sub-units — the bases, or "letters" of the genetic message. These are strung together in a long chain, and their order — the sequence — spells out the message.
● Thanks to the power of the new DNA technology, molecular biologists can now read the base sequence of DNA almost as easily as a person reads this page.
● Knowing the sequence of DNA means being able to identify where genes start and finish, being able to identify the exact position of genes that are already known, and uncover previously unknown ones. Even where the function of a gene is still unknown, the DNA sequence can be translated into its protein counterpart and give valuable clues to what it might do.
● Complete sequences are known for numerous individual genes from bacteria, plants, animals and humans, and for the genomes (all the genes) of many disease-causing viruses, whose total DNA or RNA is of the order of tens of thousands of bases long at most.
● Now molecular biologists are embarking on the mammoth task of trying to sequence the 3 billion bases that make up the human genome. Estimated cost is several hundred million dollars and the project will take anything up to 20 years.

determine what hidden defects and predispositions to this or that disease they have. Such knowledge will at the very least affect marriage and job prospects — and possibly the cost of life insurance.

Genetic correlations, if not causes, will be found for many human characteristics, such as predisposition to heart disease, or even behavioural characters such as intelligence or mental illness. Each individual could be given a genetic profile which could predict his or her medical future much better than a crystal ball. The social and legal consequences of the availability of such information will be immense.

Legislation is emerging in many countries on the issues thrown up by the new reproductive technology, but the implications of knowing more about an individual's genetic make-up have hardly been touched. This is a religious and ethical minefield for which developing countries must be well-prepared.

Meanwhile, there is the immediate issue of the prevention and treatment of infectious and parasitic diseases.

THE SILENT GENOCIDE IN THE SOUTH

In the industrialised North, most infectious and parasitic diseases have been conquered, with the striking exception of AIDS. But they still cause a "silent genocide" of children in the South, to use the phrase of the World Health Organization (WHO) Director- General, Hiroshi Nakajima.

Four million children die each year from diarrhoea; and another 2 million from measles. Some 2.7 **billion** people suffer from episodic malaria, and 1.5 million — mostly children — die of the disease each year. A billion are affected by tuberculosis, which kills nearly a million people a year. Another million die from hepatitis B [1].

As for fears about population growth if more children survive, studies show that better care for infants and mothers can lead to smaller families — as has been seen dramatically in the southern Indian state of Kerala [2].

The silent genocide could be slowed in one of three ways: by economic development; by improved delivery of existing health-care; and by the application of appropriate new research and medical technology.

Health through economic development: A hundred years ago in London, there were many deaths from malaria along the marshy banks of the River Thames; the mosquito that carried the malaria parasite can still be found in London's central green area, Hyde Park. Only decades of development, better hygiene and environmental management — such as the draining of malarial swamps — eventually rid the capital of malaria, and of many other diseases now familiar only in developing countries. Vaccines against diseases such as polio and tuberculosis, and the introduction of antibiotics also played a part.

The same revolution could happen in developing countries. But how soon? Good public hygiene — safe water and clean sanitation for all — is the most fundamental, but also the most expensive and therefore long term. Hygiene will come only as fast as overall economic development.

Improving existing health-care: For the poorest countries, vaccines and properly used drugs therefore seem to be the most practicable immediate measures to control disease. Where possible, vaccines are preferable because they can prevent disease; antibiotics and drugs can only ameliorate or cure it.

Some cheap interventions are already possible. According to Nakajima, the rate of disease and disablement in developing countries is "a preventable tragedy — because the developed world has the resources and technology to end common diseases world-wide".

Oral rehydration therapy salts for treating children with diarrhoea cost just US 10 cents a packet. Only US$50 million a year could prevent 2 million child deaths. And the wider delivery of existing cheap vaccines against polio, tetanus, measles, diphtheria, whooping cough and tuberculosis, for around US$10 a head, could save another 3 million child deaths a year.

Nevertheless, success is still far off. "Despite massive, creative educational efforts [in promoting oral rehydration therapy], diarrhoeal disease mortality has not declined substantially," says Julia Walsh, of Harvard University School of Public Health in the US [3]. And several available vaccines are difficult to deliver, requiring continuous refrigeration from the time they leave factories in the North until they reach the village. There are no vaccines yet to tackle the major tropical parasitic diseases, such as malaria, schistosomiasis or Chagas' disease.

More needs to be done just to deliver existing health-care, including some 21 high-priority products ranging from diagnostic kits to drugs, which have been developed since 1976 by the WHO Special Programme of Research and Training on Tropical Diseases (TDR). But existing vaccines and drugs need improvement; and new ones are needed for diseases that cannot yet be properly controlled.

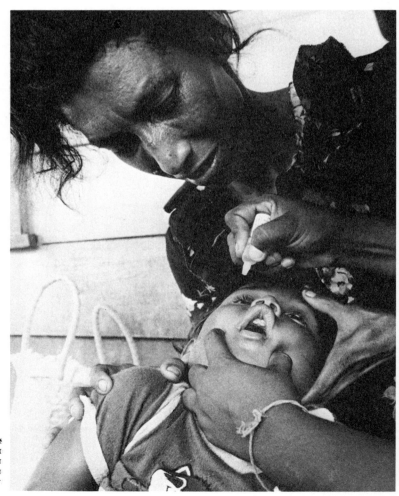

Miskito woman holds her child for oral polic vaccine during ar inoculation campaign ir Nicaragua. /*Julio Etchar*

NEW MEDICAL BIOTECHNOLOGY

B iotechnology offers no immediate cure-all for diseases that have complex economic, environmental and social causes, as well as medical ones. But it does hold some promise. Three key technologies need to be researched, developed and applied in developing country conditions: **new and improved vaccines; diagnostic kits;** and **new drugs**.

Vaccine research: the goals

"Vaccines are the most important health measure," says Walsh, because they are trebly effective — against sickness, death and transmission. Drugs and diagnostic tools have a slightly lower priority as they usually only come into play once a patient is ill. Then come environmental health and improved nutrition through crop improvement.

Vaccines also have another spin-off — they can be a stimulus to the health system. Speaking of the campaign begun in 1988 to eradicate polio, Ciro de Quadros, Latin American regional director of the Pan American Health Organization (PAHO), told Panos: "Polio is a vehicle. It will help us deliver a whole health structure."

De Quadros' experience is that programmes like WHO's Extended Programme of Immunisation, which has delivered six cheap existing vaccines to half the world's children, can, if properly managed, raise the competence, standing, and morale of local health personnel, and of the whole health service.

Carlos Castillho, representative of the United Nations Children's Fund (UNICEF) in Haiti, felt the same about the first successful vaccination days in Haiti in 1988. "Haiti had the lowest level of child immunisation in the Americas. It was very sad," he said. But the vaccination days had been "a tremendous victory — a miracle".

However, such successes need excellent organisation which is sensitive to local need, and designed to leave not just vaccines behind, but also organisational structures and new social and political attitudes and demands.

Any new vaccine must be deliverable through the primary health-care system, right through to distant villages still not served by roads, water or electricity. An ideal new vaccine for a developing country should be [4]:

- Stable at tropical temperatures for long periods (several existing ones, such as polio and measles, are not).

- Easy to administer through a cheap, disposable device not requiring sterilisation.

- Cheap, costing much less than US$1 per dose. Vaccines currently used by WHO cost only a few US cents, and any new vaccine costing more than this would have to deliver very major benefits to be affordable. (The US$1-a-dose limit is usually quoted as the highest cost at which a genetically engineered anti-hepatitis B vaccine — currently costing around $15 a dose — might become more widely available.)

- Safe, with minimal side-effects.

- Combinable with other vaccines in a single shot to make delivery as easy as possible.

- Effective work on the new-born or early infant. (Current measles vaccine can only be used later in life, complicating vaccine delivery.)

- Fast-acting, establishing immunity shortly after vaccination, to stop epidemics quickly.

It is also helpful if vaccination leaves a distinguishing mark on those who have already received the vaccine. Smallpox vaccine, for example, left a small scar on the arm or leg.

If resources can be found to research, develop and apply them, new or improved vaccines could be expected to be ready within five years for a range of bacterial and viral diseases.

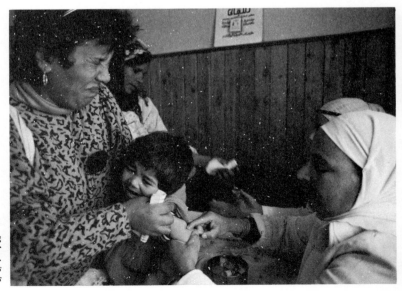

It's a life-saving immunisation shot for this child in Egypt.
/Sean Sprague/Panos Pictures

New or improved vaccines could be ready for the following in five years:

Bacteria	Viruses
Whooping cough	
(*Bordetella pertussis*)	Influenza A & B
	Hepatitis A
	Herpes simplex
Bacterial pneumonias	Parainfluenza
(*Hemophilus influenzae B &*	Rabies
Streptococcus pneumoniae)	Respiratory disease due to
Bacterial meningitis	respiratory synctial
(*Neisseria meningitidis*)	Rotavirus (a major cause of death
Typhoid fever	in childhood from diarrhoea)
(*Salmonella typhi*)	
Cholera (*Vibrio cholerae*)	

Within 10 years:

Bacteria	Viruses
Enteritis due to toxin-producing	Human immunodeficiency
Escherichia coli	(HIV, the virus that
	causes AIDS)
Leprosy (*Mycobacterium leprae*)	Japanese B encephalitis
Gonorrhoea (*Neisseria gonorrhoeae*)	
Streptococcus groups	
A & B (wound	
infections, tonsillitis, scarlet	
fever, infections during	
childbirth, sore throats	
followed by rheumatic fever, etc)	

Vaccines against malaria and other parasitic diseases are also possibilities within the next 10 years (see Chapter 7); anti-fertility vaccines for both men and women might also be developed.

Partly because of lack of research, but also because of technical difficulties, there is no prospect of an effective vaccine for some important diseases within a decade. Tuberculosis (TB), for example, is second only to malaria in affecting a billion people a year and killing nearly a million; the present 60-year-old BCG vaccine against tuberculosis is only variably successful.

A FEW BASICS... Vaccines

● Vaccines prime the immune system — the body's natural defence against infection, to react immediately to attack. They create a pre-existing state of immunity against a particular disease.
● The immune system includes the white cells of the blood, especially the lymphocytes, and tissues such as lymph nodes and spleen where lymphocytes are produced.
● The immune system works by recognising and destroying anything it perceives as "foreign". The surfaces of invading viruses, bacteria and parasites bristle with antigens. These are molecules or parts of molecules, usually of protein or carbohydrate, which the immune system recognises are not part of its own body, and which stimulate it to mount a specific attack.
● One type of lymphocyte produces antibodies — special proteins that stick to the antigen — disabling the virus or bacterium to which it belongs and making it easier for the body's scavenging system to engulf and digest it.
● Other lymphocytes become "killer" cells, attacking infected cells and destroying them directly.
● Vaccines work by mimicking an infection so that they stimulate the immune system to produce the appropriate antibodies and killer cells, but do not cause any symptoms of disease. When a real infection comes along, the body is immediately ready to respond to it and can get rid of it before the disease has time to get established and cause any damage.

Walsh selects eight areas in which vaccine research should be increased:

- Tuberculosis.

- Vaccines against respiratory diseases.

- Group B streptococcus (a major cause of maternal and infant mortality in the Third World).

- Syphilis.

- Amoebiasis.

- Immunoadjuvants (chemicals given with the simpler vaccines and designed to prod the immune system into action: they are particularly needed for the very young).

- Improving the temperature stability of old and new vaccines.

- Family-planning vaccines for men and women.

Effective vaccines for sexually transmitted diseases are also urgently needed, particularly in those parts of the world — North and South — where rapid economic and social change has altered behaviour and resulted in greater transmission, probably also carrying with it greater transmission of the HIV viruses.

Funding vaccine research

But vaccine development costs are high, and success is not always assured. Costs rise tenfold at each stage from research to development and from development to application. After identifying an effective immunising agent in animal and preliminary human trials, it will cost US$20-30 million and 7-10 years of development to arrive at a vaccine usable by ordinary paramedics in the field [5].

Private companies are thus reluctant to get into the work, as it would seem to be difficult to get a return at the prices that developing countries — or WHO — could afford. For example, the US biotechnology company Genentech had agreed to develop a promising New York University vaccine against the sporozoite stage of the malaria parasite; but it backed out when it realised the project would not be profitable [6]. Similarly, the small British biotechnology agency, Rural Investment Overseas Ltd, also considered developing vaccines against tropical diseases in the Philippines, in collaboration with the BIOTECH group of Los Banos University. However, the project was abandoned "because the market size was too small".

Other plans are afoot, however, to help developers cover the costs of development work through direct grants from outside donors (such as the United Nations Development Programme, UNDP). The vaccine producers would then sell the vaccine to WHO at production cost only. These ideas are being pressed strongly by Anthony Robbins, Professor of Public Health at the Boston University School of Medicine, and by Phyllis Freeman, Chairman of the Law Center of the College of Public and Community Services at the University of Massachusetts, also in Boston [7].

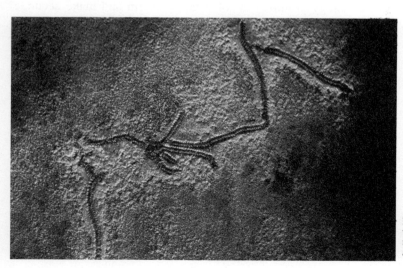

Measles virus viewed with an electron microscope. /*Science Photo Library*

In a telephone conversation early in 1990, Robbins was able to describe at least three programmes for vaccine funding as under way:

- Five Nordic and Netherlands public health bodies have established a consortium to fund vaccine development for the Third World. Balancing need with practicality, work is likely to go forward on vaccines against *Neisseria meningitidis* (meningococcus groups A & C) which has caused serious problems in Africa in recent years, and against *Streptococcus pneumoniae* (pneumococcus) — the "number one respiratory killer", according to Robbins.

- The UNDP has also promised support and will organise further fund-raising efforts.

- The Pan American Health Organisation is raising government funds for establishing regional vaccine development projects in either Mexico or Brazil.

DIAGNOSTICS

"The short-term effects of biotechnology will be in diagnostics," says Tore Godal, director of the TDR.

Correct diagnosis is essential for correct treatment, since different disease agents, requiring different treatments, can cause the same symptoms. For example, bacterial pneumonia will respond to antibiotics, whereas antibiotics are useless against pneumonia caused by a virus.

Many of today's diagnostic tests are relatively time-consuming and can only be carried out in a laboratory by highly trained technicians. Biotechnology promises to solve this problem and make accurate diagnosis much more widely available, using simple monoclonal antibody or DNA probe tests — similar to those under development for plant diseases. (DNA probes detect the disease agent's unique genetic material, monoclonal antibodies detect unique antigens on the surface of the virus, bacterium or parasite.)

Such diagnostics will also help in public health planning. Cheap surveys of the prevalence of different diseases in different areas and at different times will allow meagre health resources to be used more efficiently, and help control epidemics more quickly. DNA and antibody probes could also be used in family-planning tests for ovulation, to provide an accurate means for couples to plan their families without using contraceptives — important for Catholic communities.

DNA probes can handle large numbers of tests in one batch, so whole populations can be scanned. In Thailand, 5,000 finger-prick blood samples were scanned for malaria with a DNA probe in two days; the standard microscope-and-slide method would have taken many times longer.

In its annual report for 1987/88 [8], the TDR lists many diagnostic products which have emerged from its research programmes. "Malaria is already well-covered — and probes are being explored in all other tropical diseases covered by TDR," says Godal. Available products range from a monoclonal antibody test for the parasitic worm *Brugia malayi* (a cause of the human disease, filariasis) in its carrier insect, to synthetic peptides to test for antibodies to *Plasmodium falciparum*, a cause of malaria, to DNA probes for *Trypanosoma cruzi*, the cause of Chagas' disease.

Biotechnology is producing potential diagnostics much faster than any other medical product, partly because the problem of diagnosis is easier to tackle than that of cure or treatment — and partly because there is less need for lengthy trials of tests in animals and humans. Efficacy and safety trials may delay the introduction of a new drug or vaccine for many years, and add to costs dramatically.

But it is all very well developing a new test in the laboratory; there may be a long way to go before it can be made robust enough for field use. TDR's answer has been to establish a "biotechnology initiative" programme which is identifying indigenous researchers, laboratories and companies to develop and produce practical kits from the research ideas. This is part of TDR's increasing emphasis on the socio-economic aspects of health-care and how it may be delivered more effectively.

The biotechnology initiative, begun in mid-1989, has concentrated on local production of diagnostics. It will format the research idea into kit form, perhaps taking six months to a year to work out what is practical in the field. A preliminary scale-up to produce milligram or gram amounts of the relevant biological agent (the DNA probe, etc) for the production of, say, 10,000 kits for large-scale field testing will follow. The final step — if the tests are successful — will be full scaling-up of production to use the product in the control and monitoring programme for the disease.

Quick, cheap and simple diagnostic tests are needed to measure haemoglobin levels, test water quality, test concentrations of oral rehydration therapy salts, identify different malaria parasites and their resistances to drugs, and identify different respiratory pathogens.

The connection between infections in pregnancy and low birth-weight babies also needs to be studied. Eliminating low birth-weight should save 5 million lives annually. Similarly, the causes of maternal

Waiting for the doctor at a village clinic in Bangladesh. */Cooper and Hammond/Panos Pictures*

Waiting for the doctor at a village clinic in Bangladesh. /Cooper and Hammond/Panos Pictures

mortality (500,000 deaths annually, with serious consequences for whole families) should be investigated. In both cases, better scientific understanding of causes should lead to more effective health strategies and treatments.

NEW DRUGS

For pharmaceuticals, as with vaccines, the objective of research should be to find a drug which is effective in a single dose, has few adverse reactions, is cheap, and is easily administered in primary health-care systems.

New drugs are particularly needed against tuberculosis, against viruses, and against parasites.

Promising new drugs include the interferons and interleukins, which stimulate the immune system, helping the body to fight infection. These are true products of the new biotechnology. They are human proteins that cannot be produced in any useful amount except from genetically engineered bacteria into which the relevant human genes have been transplanted.

Molecular biology has also helped to identify a possible new drug against one of the two forms of African trypanosomiasis (sleeping sickness). Difluoromethyl ornithine blocks a precise metabolic pathway in the trypanosome which causes West African sleeping sickness, without harming the patient's own cells.

As for the production and delivery of such drugs at low cost, the TDR's biotechnology initiative could help. Another model, expressly for encouraging local antibiotic production, is one developed by the UK-based Biotics Ltd for approval by the European Commission. Called the "Regional Antibiotics Manufacturing Project" (RAMP), it envisages joint antibiotic-making ventures between regional groups of developing countries, established pharmaceutical companies and international donors. The plants would be built in developing countries at the donors' cost; the country would provide labour, raw materials — for example, molasses — and a guaranteed local market, and gain jobs and a technology; the pharmaceutical company would gain a new source of supply at zero capital cost [10].

Some scientific strategies for developing new drugs are discussed in the next chapter.

MICRONUTRIENTS

In many regions there are deficiencies of micronutrients (vitamins and trace elements needed in small amounts for health). Lack of vitamin A causes 500,000 cases of corneal blindness and 5 million cases of non-corneal xerophthalmia — a thickening of the eye-ball — among pre-school children. Research is showing the key role of vitamin A in diminishing mortality from, and occurrence of, common tropical diseases and certain cancers.

Some 800 million people live in areas deficient in iodine —

essential for normal growth and development, particularly of the brain of the unborn child, as recent research has shown. Iron deficiency is also widespread among reproductive women and young children.

Biotechnology might help by developing crops with improved take-up of micronutrients, or production of vitamins. Work is in progress on a rice with more vitamin A.

DISEASE VECTORS

The control of disease vectors — the insects, snails and other organisms that carry disease from one human host to another — will also be improved by an integrated approach using all the tools of modern biology together with public education.

Improvements can range from simple filling in puddles and turning over cans to prevent the growth of mosquito larvae, to the selection, possible engineering and release of bacteria, viruses, insects and other organisms that will prey on disease vectors. New, less toxic, and more effective chemical insecticides and control strategies may also be developed, using detailed understanding of specific insect metabolism and behaviour. Chemical substitutes mimicking the odour of the breath of oxen can attract tsetse flies to insecticidal traps from kilometres away [11].

FIELD TRIALS

After funding, the greatest hurdle may be clinical trials of new drugs and vaccines, since they require large, carefully followed populations and experienced field study teams, and sometimes must

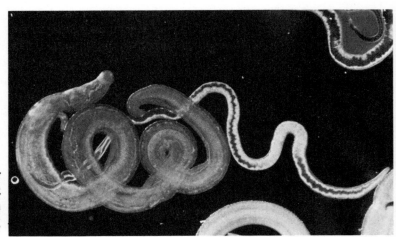

Light micrograph of *Schistosoma mansoi*, the cause of schistosomiasis in adult intestinal blood. */Science Photo Library*

be carried out in poorly accessible areas. In pursuing such trials it will be essential to have not only funds, but also the willing compliance of the population and the active help of the local health, media and political forces.

Full-scale trials are already needed to test various drugs. Several places already conduct excellent field epidemiological studies and can serve as models for others, such as the International Centre of Diarrhoeal Disease Research in Bangladesh; the UK's Medical Research Laboratory in Gambia; the respiratory disease and malaria field sites in Papua New Guinea; and the Kasongo Primary Health Care Project in Zaire.

ATTRACTING SCIENTISTS

TDR specialises in seven important groups of diseases where scientists from the industrial world could be persuaded to do work by virtue of the scientific interest of the problem. These are malaria, schistosomiasis, leprosy, the filariases, African trypanosomiasis, Chagas' disease, and the leishmaniases.

Many Northern scientists have turned to tropical diseases because they offer great scientific challenges. For example, the organisms that cause sleeping sickness (African trypanosomiasis) change their protein coats with bewildering speed to fool the body's defences. Because of the genetic interest of this problem, many molecular biologists are studying sleeping sickness.

The Latin American Chagas' disease, which leads to great disability later in life, is caused by a related organism, *Trypanosoma cruzi*. But it is less well studied, arguably because it is less interesting to molecular biologists: *T. cruzi* does not change its coat.

Leprosy also fascinates some scientists, quite apart from its medical importance, because of its apparent ability to turn off the immune system. Barry Bloom, a leading leprosy researcher in New York, has said that when he started "it was hard to find six people for a meeting. Now it's almost a cottage industry."

Developing country scientists are also at work. Victor Nussenzweig, malaria specialist at New York Unversity, says his work would not have been possible without his collaborators at the University of São Paulo, Brazil, and elsewhere. Colombian researcher Professor Pattaroyo has developed his own trial malaria vaccine. Sri Lanka also boasts excellent malaria research.

The impact of molecular biology and biotechnology on tropical disease is already not negligible, and is increasing rapidly. Some of this research is detailed in the next chapter and in reference [14].

FOCUS ON FIGURES:
Third World diseases

The main Third World diseases kill millions each year:

- Acute respiratory infections kill an estimated 10 million a year, mostly babies and children.

- Circulatory ailments (including diabetes): 8 million.

- Low birth-weight (as a major cause of other infections): 5 million.

- Diarrhoea: 4 million.

- Measles: 67 million cases a year, causing 2 million deaths.

- Injuries: 2 million.

- Malnutrition (as a major cause of other infections): 2 million.

- Cancer: 1.7 million.

- Tetanus: 1.2 million.

- Malaria: 107 million cases a year, causing 1.5 million deaths.

- Tuberculosis: 1 billion cases a year, causing 900,000 deaths.

- Hepatitis B: 300 million cases a year, causing 800,000 deaths.

- Whooping cough: 600,000.

- Typhoid: 600,000.

- Death of mothers in child-bearing: 500,000.

- Meningitis: 350,000.

- Schistosomiasis: endemic in 76 countries, with 600 million people at risk of infection, and 200 million infected, causing some 200,000 deaths a year.

- Syphilis: 15 million cases a year, causing 200,000 deaths.

- Amoebiasis: 500 million cases, causing 70,000 deaths.

- AIDS: 4 million HIV infections, causing 50,000-70,000 deaths

- Chagas' disease (American trypanosomiasis): 90 million at risk in Latin America, 16-18 million people infected, causing many thousands of deaths. In some areas of Brazil, 10% of all adult deaths are due to this disease.

- Rheumatic fever and heart disease: 52,000.

- Hookworm (an intestinal parasite): 800 million cases, causing 50,000 deaths.

- Rabies: 35,000 cases, usually fatal because of unavailability of the standard vaccine treatment.

- Diphtheria: 60 million cases, 30,000 deaths.

- Dengue: 15,000.

- Hepatitis A: 14,000.

- Yellow fever: 9,000.

- Japanese B encephalitis: 7,000.

- Ascariasis (intestinal worms up to 40 cm long): 1 billion cases, under 10,000 deaths, but 300,000 cases a year require surgical treatment.

- Giardiasis (intestinal protozoal infection): 250 million cases, under 10,000 deaths.

- Polio: 150 million cases, 2,000 deaths.

- Leprosy: 10-12 million people infected, 1,000 deaths (through indirect effects such as ulceration).

- The leishmaniases: 12 million infected, more than 400,000 new cases each year; the last epidemic of the fatal form, "visceral" leishmaniasis, caused 20,000 deaths in India in 1977-8.

- Trichuriasis (5-cm worm communicated by cats and dogs): estimated 500 million cases, with unknown numbers suffering from blindness or neurological disorders; under 1,000 deaths.

- Elephantiasis (lymphatic filariasis): 900 million at risk, 90 million infected, under 1,000 deaths.

- River blindness (onchocerciasis): endemic in 34 countries of Africa and Latin America; 90 million at risk of infection, 18 million cases, and 330,000 blinded by the disease.

- Guinea worm (dracunculiasis): 1 million cases, under 1,000 deaths (from infection of the skin ulcers caused by the metre-long worm).

- Sleeping sickness (African trypanosomiasis): endemic in 36 sub-Saharan African countries in the tsetse belt, with 50 million people living in 200 foci of the disease. Some 25,000 new cases are reported each year but the real incidence is "certainly much higher" (WHO). If untreated, the disease is invariably fatal.

Source: From Walsh [12], updated where available with latest estimates from the WHO Tropical Disease Research Programme [13] and the WHO World Report on Tropical Diseases 1990 (WHO Features).

CHAPTER 7

MAKING NEW VACCINES AND DRUGS

After diagnostic tests (see Chapter 6), new vaccines and drugs are probably biotechnology's main potential contribution to the health problems of developing countries. But what scientific strategies can biotechnologists follow? And what might they do for three key tropical diseases — malaria, Chagas' disease and leprosy?

VACCINES AND THE IMMUNE SYSTEM

Vaccines prime the body's natural defence against disease — the immune system — to react immediately to attack. They create a pre-existing state of immunity against a particular disease. In order to develop effective vaccines against diseases which have proved resistant to previous efforts, new methods of outwitting the disease agents have to be found.

The immune system

The immune system works by destroying anything it perceives as "foreign". It is distributed throughout the body and includes the white cells of the blood, the lymphocytes in particular, and lymphoid tissues such as lymph nodes and spleen, where lymphocytes are produced.

The two executive arms of the immune system, both of which must usually be activated to produce an effective response against disease, are the B-lymphocyte or B-cell system, which produces antibodies, and the T-lymphocyte or T-cell system, which helps B-cells make antibodies, and also produces activated "killer" T- cells that kill virus- or parasite-infected body cells by direct contact.

Immunity due to antibodies is relatively well understood. But the cell-mediated immunity due to the T-cell system still holds many mysteries even though it is deeply involved in the body's response to many tropical diseases. An improved understanding of cell-mediated immunity may be necessary to develop effective vaccines against tropical diseases, and the use of gene cloning and other new techniques in immunological research is helping to achieve this.

Cell-mediated immunity involving killer T-cells is particularly important in diseases in which the parasite, be it virus, bacterium or larger parasite, spends most of its life inside the host's cells. Such diseases include malaria, HIV infection, and some bacterial diseases such as gonorrhoea. Antibodies are very effective at mopping up viruses and bacteria that are circulating freely in the blood or in the fluids between cells, but once a pathogen gets inside a cell it is often hidden from this part of the immune system.

Rational vaccine design

Most disease-causing organisms (pathogens) generate some degree of natural immunity in the individual, but sometimes not before a great

A FEW BASICS... antigens and antibodies

● Antigens are any molecules or parts of molecules (usually of protein or carbohydrate) which the immune system recognises as foreign, and which stimulate it to mount a specific attack. Some antigens stimulate an antibody response, whereas others preferentially stimulate the T-cell system.
● An immune response mounted against one antigen only confers immunity against that antigen. So a vaccine against polio, for example, only confers immunity against polio.
● Conserved antigens are critical for the design of vaccines. Many parasites, in particular, are continually changing the antigenic face they present to the immune system. But some antigens, often part of an invader's fundamental attack and entry system, do not change. If a strong immune response against such conserved antigens can be mounted, there is a better chance of setting up useful immunity to the invader.
● Antibodies, or immunoglobulins, are large proteins which recognise and stick to antigens, disabling them and making it easier for the body's scavenging system to get rid of them. Each type of antibody has a distinct shape that only fits one, or a very few, antigens.
● B-cells make antibodies. There are millions of different B-cells in the human body. Each B-cell and all its descendants makes just one type of antibody.
● T-cells don't make antibodies. Some T-cells ("helper" T-cells) recognise invaders and stimulate antibody production by the appropriate B-cells. "Killer" T-cells recognise and destroy the patient's own cells that have become altered by infection with virus, bacteria or parasites, and which are displaying some "foreign" antigen on their surface. Some T-cells are "suppressor" cells, actually preventing the immune system mounting an attack against a particular antigen. Each T-cell and all its descendants is specific for just one type of antigen. Immunity mediated by the T-cell system is often known as cell-mediated immunity, as it is produced by the direct action of T-cells.
● Immunogenicity is the degree to which something actually stimulates an effective immune response. Often the main problem with vaccine design comes not in including the right antigens, but in increasing their immunogenicity to a sufficient level to be useful to the patient.
● Adjuvants are sometimes used to increase the immunogenicity of a vaccine. They are non-specific materials (such as aluminium oxide) which increase the strength of an immune response to any vaccine. A well-known adjuvant is the coat of the bacterium "Bacille Calmette-Guerin" (BCG) used in the BCG vaccine against tuberculosis.

deal of damage has been done during the course of the illness.

In some diseases, a quite long-lasting immunity develops after only one infection, so illness caused by a second encounter is much less severe or non-existent. Vaccines against this type of pathogen are relatively easy to produce and many already exist. Examples are polio, smallpox, measles, typhoid and influenza. They make use of either the killed micro-organism, or a live but weakened and harmless strain.

With other diseases, natural immunity develops only after a long series of infections, as in malaria, where it develops in late childhood and adulthood among those who have survived repeated attacks. This type of disease is much more difficult to protect against by vaccination.

In yet other cases, the invading organism appears to be able to avoid or seriously suppress the immune reaction (as in leprosy or AIDS). These present perhaps an even greater challenge.

Relatively few vaccines have been really successful. The prime examples are those against smallpox, which eliminated the disease from the globe, and polio, which is well on the way towards the same end. The trouble has been that vaccine design has been a rather trial-and-error process, depending on the chance availability of weakened strains of the pathogen, or on the effectiveness of killed preparations.

But vaccine design is coming of age. Biotechnology can aid rational vaccine design in several ways.

Sub-unit vaccines

Gene cloning offers the possibility of mass-producing any antigen without the need to grow large amounts of live virus or bacteria. Instead of having to use the whole microbe in some form, vaccines can now be prepared from just the relevant antigens. This type of so-called sub-unit vaccine allows the immunologist to pick and choose exactly which antigens go into the vaccines, and it also makes the business of vaccine production much safer. One of the vaccines recently developed against hepatitis B is of this type, with the appropriate antigen being mass-produced from cloned hepatitis virus genes.

Once an antigen gene has been cloned it can be dissected in molecular detail to find out which part of the antigen is best at stimulating a particular type of immune response. Some antigens tend to stimulate antibody production, whereas others are better at stimulating cell-mediated immunity. "Artificial" antigens consisting of the most effective parts of several different molecules can now be constructed if needed.

A drawback of sub-unit vaccines as a class is that the antigen proteins on their own are often not very successful at stimulating a strong enough immune response. One way of overcoming this is to mix them with immunoadjuvants, materials that are not themselves antigens but which make the antigen more effective.

Genetically engineered vaccines

Another way of presenting an antigen effectively to the immune system is to engineer it into a live carrier virus or bacterium. The carrier is a harmless or disabled strain of some well-known micro-organism. Vaccinia virus, which was used to immunise the world against smallpox, is the main virus developed as a carrier so far. Salmonella and BCG bacteria have also been thought of as carriers.

Genes that might make the carrier harmful are removed, and

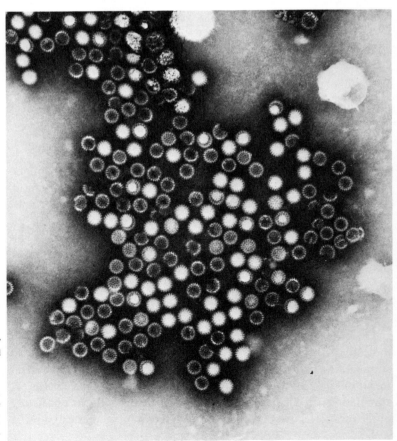

A cluster of protein-studded rotavirus, the tiny virus that causes a lethal diarrhoea in children. Vaccines against rotavirus are under development.
/Dr E.H. Cook/Science Photo Library

replaced with genes specifying the required antigens. Engineered vaccinia has already been used to generate immunity in animals to rabies, herpes simplex, influenza and hepatitis B. But some argue against its use in humans because of a relatively high rate of adverse reactions to vaccinia and its possible reversion to a smallpox-type virus.

Genetic engineering can also be used to produce a vaccine strain of micro-organism directly from a pathogen by altering or removing some harmful gene, while leaving behind the genes for useful antigens. Such weakened microbes will not cause disease, but, it is hoped, will stimulate immunity against the real thing.

The final costs of any vaccine are fundamental to its practicability. Nothing over US$1 a treatment seems possible in developing countries whose annual health budgets per person might be little more than that. Current childhood vaccines used by the Extended Programme of Immuniaztion (EPI) of the World Health Organization (WHO) cost only a few US cents.

RATIONAL DRUGS

Historically, drug development has been somewhat random. Thousands of compounds are initially tested on animals, to see what effect they have on "model" diseases. Chemical modifications are made to the more promising ones in an attempt to improve performance. A whole series of careful human trials may begin. Only a few drugs finally prove useful.

But now a new phase of drug design is beginning. With greater understanding of disease organisms, and the body's reaction to them, it is becoming possible to engage in rational drug design — targeting the organisms' weak spots. This is another new area of work where the UNDP/World Bank/WHO's Tropical Disease Research Programme (TDR) aims to put in increasing effort.

A pathogen's weak spots are most likely to be fundamental chemical strategies which it uses during its life in the body — such as the molecular mechanism whereby the malaria parasite invades a red blood cell. If (cheap) drugs could be designed to block these processes while leaving the human host unaffected, the parasites would be effectively controlled.

Strategies for drug design will certainly emerge out of the research that is now going on towards the development of vaccines against several tropical diseases — such as malaria. In fact, many scientists now believe that the first useful results of such work will not be vaccines at all, but precisely targeted drugs.

The production of engineered vaccines is not simple. Here, a laboratory technician prepares a fermentation unit for growth of yeast cells, genetically engineered to produce coat-proteins of the hepatitis B virus. These proteins are extracted to make a vaccine against hepatitis B.

Novel drugs that boost the immune system are one area of great interest. The immune system is the body's own defence against invasion and drugs must be designed to help, and not hinder it.

Interferons and interleukins are two classes of such drugs. They are proteins produced by the immune system during immune responses to invading organisms, and their normal role is to help gear up the immune system to attack. Some interferons also have a direct anti-viral effect.

Interferons may already be showing their worth against tropical diseases, according to evidence presented at a conference on the drugs in Havana, Cuba, in April 1989. At that meeting, French and Brazilian scientists presented "dramatic success" in treating the parasitic disease, leishmaniasis (in which a single-celled protozoan parasite, Leishmania, infects the body's internal organs), with gamma-interferon, one of the three main types of interferon.

This drug reactivated a depressed immune response to the disease in 17 patients, who appeared "cured" after just 10 days of treatment. Interleukin 2 was reported to reactivate an immune response against advanced leprosy [1].

As interferon, interleukin and other similar proteins can only be practicably produced from genetically engineered bacteria, their development as drugs has depended entirely on the advent of recombinant DNA.

BEATING MALARIA

Malaria affects at least 2.7 billion people in developing countries. In Vietnam, more Americans are said to have died from malaria than in combat.

Moreover, the numbers of ordinary people affected by malaria are growing rapidly after the efforts, using DDT, in the 1950s and 1960s to eradicate the mosquito carriers of the disease proved unsustainable in poor communities. This exercise, which could not be maintained for reasons of cost and logistics, led to the development of pesticide resistance in the mosquitoes.

"We thought we could beat malaria with a little bit of insecticide," said Halfdan Mahler, who retired in 1988 as WHO Director-General. "But we didn't realise the mosquito was such a nasty damn insect, that it would adjust so well and develop resistance. We were far too optimistic [2]."

More recently, some malaria organisms themselves have developed resistance to several of the most widely used drug treatments. Even where drugs are available to be taken "prophylactically" (that is, before infection, to kill the organisms immediately they are encountered), infection rates are not greatly reduced (for example, from 100% to 80% in Ethiopia). This is partly because people stop taking the tablets after a few weeks, and partly because in many areas of the world there are long climatic seasons when drug distribution is impossible or severely reduced.

Previously, malaria was usually lethal only in childhood, in regions where the disease was endemic. But now non-immune adults "are dying in large numbers," says one expert.

The causes are the transmigration of people with no previous malaria exposure, and so no resistance, into malarial areas — as in the resettlement programme in Ethiopia, or the increasing sapphire mining on the Thai-Cambodian border. Added to this is world-wide forest clearance and dam building, creating new ponds, puddles and lakes suitable for mosquito breeding.

One approach to lowering the death rate might be to aim at halting the spread of malaria to the brain, as "cerebral malaria" is the most lethal condition. It is caused by parasite-packed blood cells lodging in the walls of the small arteries of the brain. "Death is quick," when this condition sets in, says David Warrell, Professor of Tropical Medicine at the University of Oxford, England, who has treated the disease in Thailand. New fast-acting, safe, injectable drugs are needed. Chloroquine used to be good, but in Thailand the parasites have high-grade resistance.

The exact death rate world-wide from malaria is not easy to estimate. It is not only a killer in itself, but depresses resistance to other diseases, and so may lead to deaths usually recorded in other categories.

Speaking at a WHO meeting in June 1989, Dr Brian Greenwood of the UK's Medical Research Council centre in The Gambia, estimated that, each year, around 460,000 Africans die directly as a result of malaria fevers. Some 420,000 (90%) of these deaths occur in the forests and savannahs. The indirect deaths from malaria are probably double this, he said: nearly one million a year in Africa alone.

Moreover, according to the annual report of the TDR, to a child, "malaria represents a serious risk, not just to survival, but also to growth, fitness and educational achievement".

Meanwhile, the military, business and tourist interest in protecting Northerners in their visits to the South has attracted large sums to malaria research, in which biotechnology is deeply involved. According to figures collected by the US Office of Technology Assessment, an independent research bureau of the US Congress, 21% of all WHO and US spending on tropical diseases research went to malaria — some US$23 million. Of this, over US$19 million came from US sources, of which in turn over US$4 million was military money, much of it focusing on research at the Walter Reed Army Hospital in Washington DC, aimed at protecting US troops in tropical combat zones.

Questions may legitimately be raised whether such high-tech research will lead to appropriate treatments for developing country conditions: for example, will any vaccines arising be cheap enough? Could the money be better spent on environmental control? But WHO observers believe there will be useful results from this research and that it must be monitored and encouraged to move in appropriate directions.

Malaria vaccines

Will a malaria vaccine ever be possible? Probably yes, in the long run, as it is clear that people exposed to malaria do slowly develop resistance. The problems are: how to speed up that natural process; how to deliver effective immunity with — at the very best — a single shot of vaccine; and how to ensure the resulting vaccine is cheap and easy to deliver in field conditions.

However, projections in the mid-1980s that a vaccine would be available by 1990 have proved far too optimistic. It seems that the strategy that works for hepatitis B — to make a vaccine containing the coat proteins, to stimulate protective antibodies — is not enough for tropical parasites, and second lines of attack are now required. The key may be to develop strong T-cell immunity as well.

A FEW BASICS... the malaria parasite

Malaria is caused by several species of single-celled, microscopic, protozoan parasites of the genus *Plasmodium*, which are transmitted by the bite of an anopheline mosquito.

Four main *Plasmodium* species cause malaria: *P. falciparum*, *P. vivax*, *P. malariae*, and *P. ovale*, each with its own slightly different antigens, form, disease-effects and relationships with mosquitoes. *P. falciparum* is the most common in tropical and sub-tropical areas, the most virulent species, and the main killer.

P. vivax is the most widely distributed, reaching into temperate areas, but is less virulent than *falciparum*. It can cause relapses up to three years after infection.

P. malariae, widely distributed but less common than the other species, can cause relapses up to 30 years after infection.

P. ovale is found mostly in tropical Africa, and causes relapses up to five years after infection.

The malaria life-cycle has several stages. Each stage requires a different strategy of attack by drugs or vaccines, because it presents the immune system with different antigens.

It begins with sporozoites in the mosquito gut and saliva. These enter the human bloodstream through the bite of an infected mosquito. But within 30 minutes they have left the blood and entered the liver cells, where they hide from immune system attack.

In the liver, the sporozoites multiply and change into merozoites which eventually burst out in their thousands into the bloodstream. They enter the red blood cells, and go through several stages before producing a new burst of merozoites, destroying their host cells in unison and infecting more. Each such burst, which takes place every one to three days according to the species involved, causes a new fever in the patient, creating the characteristic one- to three-day cycles of malaria fever.

Eventually, the parasites produce yet another form in the blood, male and female gametocytes. These are taken up by a biting mosquito, and combine in the gut to make sporozoites again, thus restarting the infection cycle.

The bite that kills children and the unprotected – a malaria-transmitting mosquito. /*Nigel Cattlin/Holt Studios Ltd*

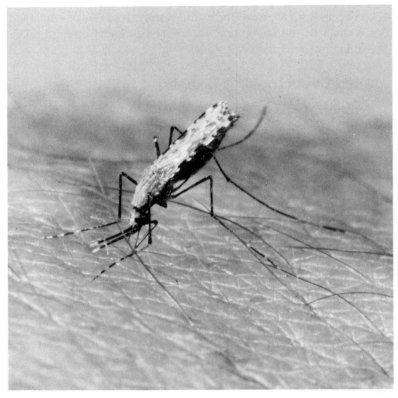

There have also been recent problems with alleged corruption in the US malaria research funding programme, which has hindered effective research planning, and a big investigation into the state of malaria research has been under way [3].

Meanwhile, molecular biology has been involved most intimately in developing vaccines against *P. falciparum*, the leading killer.

Victor and Ruth Nussenzweig of the New York University School of Medicine had singled out the sporozoite stage of malaria for vaccine attack because experiments vaccinating volunteers with whole, killed irradiated sporozoites had produced effective immunity. (The technique was not practicable for other than experimental use, however.) Also, it was clear that killing sporozoites would prevent all disease symptoms.

Trials with a vaccine made from an antigen from the sporozoite surface protein, the "circumsporozoite" or CS protein, that stimulated B-cell antibody production, proved disappointing, however, with only partial immunity being produced in a few individuals. Moreover, in one important strain of malaria, caused by *P. vivax*, it was discovered that the CS protein was variable — so a vaccine made against one form of it would not be effective against most others [4].

However, scientists at the Walter Reed Army Hospital and the Swiss Serum and Vaccine Institute in Berne tried another route. They took disabled Salmonella bacteria — ones whose genes for making gastric toxins have been removed — and engineered into them genes expressing malaria sporozoite CS protein antigens. Such a vaccine could be taken orally. The resulting construct proved effective against malaria in mice without stimulating antibodies at all. It must therefore have been working solely by generating cell-mediated immunity.

The Nussenzweigs, together with colleagues in Switzerland, identified an antigen on the CS protein that produced this T-cell response in mice [5]. Conceivably, a vaccine based on this antigen, together with the previous antigen that stimulated antibodies, will prove more effective. But it is a long way from mice to people.

According to Victor Nussenzweig, a sporozoite vaccine "will be perfected gradually". The "brightest and best immunologists are thinking of vaccines," he says.

Vaccines against merozoites and other blood stages are also being developed along similar lines, looking for conserved antigens which stimulate both antibody and T-cell immunity.

Another approach involves stimulating attacks on liver cells which have been invaded by sporozoites; the infected cells display "foreign" malaria antigens on their surface which the immune system may be persuaded to recognise and attack.

Anti-malarial drugs

Drugs are perhaps closer to the front line of attack on malaria, if only because the parasites are developing resistance to the existing treatments, and drugs are generally easier to create — and to deliver — than vaccines.

Classical techniques for developing new drugs continue alongside more modern methods, and there are hopes for artemisinin (qinghaosu), a traditional Chinese remedy extracted from wormwood, which has halved the malaria death rate in China. Other potential drugs include halofantrine, though multiple doses were needed for cure in Thai trials; mefloquine, though this appears to cause some (reversible) mental disorder in 1-2% of patients; and combinations of these and other drugs in different dose regimes.

Drug-resistant malaria

One line of research has been to identify, and counter, the parasite's method for resisting the known and previously effective drugs — in particular, chloroquine. The drug-resistant parasites seem to be using a strategy also used by "multiple drug resistant" cancer cells. These cells increase the number of surface pores that pump out any toxic molecules entering the cell. The cell is able to keep the drug concentration inside low, and so survives.

It may be possible therefore to design a supplementary drug, to be given with chloroquine, that will block those pores in the parasite.

Verapamil is one such drug, but unfortunately has unwanted effects on the heart. Its modification is being attempted to remove these undesirable side-effects. And a search is now on among anti-cancer drugs, particularly those known to block the multiple drug-resistance system, for an effective substitute.

Two *P. falciparum* genes specifying multiple drug-resistance are being studied, and an understanding of their action should help speed an attack on drug-resistant malaria.

Other molecular approaches involve drugs designed to block the system which the parasite uses to garner haemoglobin, and thus oxygen, from the blood, or drugs to stop red blood cells, once they are infected with merozoites, sticking to the walls of blood vessels, often in the brain. The latter would help to reduce lethal cerebral malaria.

Malaria diagnosis

For the present, a microscope is the main method for diagnosing malaria, whether in people or in a population of mosquitoes. Such diagnosis needs trained microscopists, and is difficult, inaccurate, lengthy and expensive. But the picture is changing, as new methods are being applied, including the use of DNA probes (which latch on specifically to parasite DNA) and monoclonal antibodies (which recognise unique antigens on the parasite surface).

- Radioactively labelled DNA probes (which ideally need a regional source of radio-isotopes, or regular imports, as the radioactivity decays in a few weeks and must be handled safely) to identify *P. falciparum* have been successfully field-tested in Kenya and Thailand. According to the Tropical Disease Research Programme, the method appears suitable for epidemiology (measuring the frequency and distribution of the disease over an area) to aid the design of malaria control programmes. DNA probes are still too slow, however, to be useful for individual diagnosis. They take several hours to produce results.

- Non-radioactive DNA probes (which are easier to store and use in developing country conditions), in which the probe is "dyed" rather than made radioactive, but which may be less sensitive, have also been developed and are being compared with the radio-active probes.

- DNA probes are being developed to identify drug-resistant parasites. The probe sequences will be constructed so that they recognise parts of the recently discovered *P. falciparum* multiple drug-resistance genes.

- The polymerase chain reaction, which can copy a piece of DNA a million-fold in the test-tube, is being used to look for mutant genes in resistant parasites, and to study the global distribution of resistance.

- Monoclonal antibody probes are being field-tested for the detection of *P. falciparum* and *P. vivax* sporozoites in mosquitoes. According to WHO, they are proving valuable for estimating the degree of transmission and for identifying the particular types of mosquito that are important in transmitting the disease. In Brazil and Sri Lanka, eight new and unexpected mosquito vectors were found [6]. The monoclonal antibody technique has also shown that some mosquitoes carry only *falciparum* or only *vivax* malaria, while others carry both. Kits for the detection of *P. malariae* and *P. ovale* sporozoites are also being prepared.

Malaria vector control

Control of mosquitoes using DDT was the first major attack on malaria. Although it succeeded in eliminating malaria from areas of the globe inhabited by 1.5 billion people, it failed in many poor areas for several reasons, from unsustainable costs to the fact that mosquito populations evolved which had resistance to DDT; other mosquitoes lived in parts of the habitat that escaped being sprayed.

One of the latest control techniques seems simple and primitive, but for the moment it works: the use of bed nets impregnated with insecticides such as pyrethroids. These have been effective in reducing malaria in The Gambia, Burkina Faso, and Hainan Island in China. It may also prove possible to genetically engineer mosquitoes so they are unable to carry, and so transmit, the malaria parasite.

Molecular biology is showing that the vectors of malaria are much more complex than previously thought. Several mosquito "species" are turning out to be collections of sub-species that may look identical, but actually have widely different feeding and breeding behaviours — and degrees of insecticide resistance — that would grossly affect the choice of appropriate malaria transmission and control measures.

CHAGAS' DISEASE

Chagas' disease is a disease of poverty from Mexico to southern Argentina, caused by the single-celled protozoan parasite *Trypanosoma cruzi*, and carried from person to person by triatomine bugs which live in the crevices of mud-walled houses.

In some valleys of Bolivia, seven out of 10 people have the disease; throughout the affected countries, some 16-18 million are believed infected. Charles Darwin, the famed 19th century biologist who formulated the theory of evolution, was himself a possible victim of the disease: he suffered serious ill-health ever after his voyage around the coast of Latin America to the Galapagos islands.

The disease begins with a short acute fever, which causes most deaths; then, in survivors, it goes quiet for up to 15 years, when in half the cases it leads to increasing destruction of the heart and digestive system. The main social burden of the disease comes with the disabilities of these affected survivors.

Drugs and vaccines for Chagas' disease

There are no effective drugs or vaccines to deal with the disease. Or at least, not yet. The disease is under-researched. Nevertheless, among biotechnological approaches, Frank Ashell's work at Imperial College, London, and related approaches, may hold out promise.

Ashell and his collaborator Catherine Lowndes are working with trypanosome proteases, enzymes that destroy other proteins.

The trypanosome probably uses its proteases to cut a way into the target cells. Ashell and Lowndes have found several specific proteases, unique to the Chagas trypanosome, which might be targets for drugs designed to inhibit protease action.

"It's easy to inhibit proteases," says Ashell. But the trick will be to design or find an inhibitor that blocks only trypanosome proteases, and not those of the host, and in sufficient strength to kill or disable the whole parasite.

An alternative technique is to design drugs specifically to block a peptide (also found in African trypanosomes and the related leishmania) called trypanothione, essential to the cell, and not found in other organisms. Drugs narrowly targeted against trypanothione would be a great step forward in the treatment of all three diseases.

Diagnosis

Specific DNA probes are being developethat can identify the very variable *T. cruzi* parasite . They will probably target DNA unique to trypanosomes, and highly conserved between varieties, part of the

DNA of a subcellular organette — the kinetoplast.

Good probes will be useful not only for diagnosis and epidemiology, but also for testing South American blood in regional blood banks, which, as a result of unregulated commercial blood collection, can be infected with the disease (as well as with HIV virus, hepatitis B and syphilis).

LEPROSY

Leprosy is caused by the bacterium *Mycobacterium leprae*, which belongs to the same genus as *M. tuberculosis*, the cause of tuberculosis. It thrives in cool tissues, which is why it affects and disfigures body extremities — the nose, hands, and feet.

Drugs for leprosy

With some 5 million registered patients, and probably more than that number unregistered and untreated, leprosy control has long been faced with the increasing resistance of *M. leprae* to its principal treatment, the drug dapsone. Drug treatment is often needed for life,

Vaccination in Tamil-Nadu, Southern India – potentially, the cheapest way to provide good health.
/Ron Giling/Panos Pictures

and many sufferers are reluctant to attend clinics and so announce their status as lepers.

But sensitive clinic management, and a very successful multiple drug therapy in which dapsone is combined with the antibiotic rifampicin, or some substitute, gives new hope. Multiple drug treatment can clear the organism from the body in six months for the early stage of the disease, and in two years for later stages — the period, which does not occur in all patients, when the body's cell-mediated immunity to leprosy fails.

Multiple drug therapy has been described as a miracle treatment. No relapses have been detected, even after such short treatment, in "8,000 patient-years of observation" in India, says TDR [7]. In Malawi, the therapy has reduced incidence of the disease (in registered patients) by 70-80% .

So far, only 20% of the estimated number of sufferers world-wide have been reached with multi-drug therapy, because of cost and distribution problems. But WHO specialists predict that registered cases will be halved by 1995, and only a quarter the present number will be left by the end of the century.

"But dealing with the remainder of cases will be much harder," said one expert. "Then we shall need a vaccine. And it looks as if it is coming when it is needed, at the end of the century."

Vaccines for leprosy

The existing BCG vaccine against tuberculosis also has some effect on leprosy, as the organisms are similar. It is cheap but only variably effective. A new vaccine prepared by culturing *M. leprae* in nine-banded armadillos (one of the few animals other than humans in which leprosy will grow) and extracting and killing the bacteria, is now under a decade-long trial in Malawi and Venezuela. Trials with a vaccine prepared from a related bacterium are in progress in Bombay. But such vaccines, even if successful, will be difficult to prepare and administer in large quantities.

Genetic engineering could play a part in vaccine development by transferring *M. leprae* genes into the BCG organism so that it would express *M. leprae* antigens on its surface, perhaps making present BCG vaccines more effective against leprosy. A search for the genes coding for immune-stimulating antigens is under way.

Success, however, requires development of effective DNA carriers to transfer the genes into BCG. Gene transfer has been accomplished into another related species, *M. smegmatis*; BCG may be next.

Diagnosis

Barry Bloom, the New York scientist responsible for much of the armadillo work, says biotechnology should be used to develop simple diagnostic tests, so patents can be identified early, and perhaps in routine screening, in local clinics [8]. Because too few people develop antibodies against *M. leprae* — the usual way of identifying those infected — probes are needed to detect the bacterium itself.

CHAPTER 8

GENETIC ENGINEERING OF MICRO-ORGANISMS

THE USEFUL MICROBE

Although the users didn't know it, microbes (mostly bacteria and fungi) have been used throughout history for preserving and improving foods and drinks, and for fertilising fields. Nowadays, they are also the source of antibiotics and other pharmaceuticals; they are used to control insects; and moreover, with genetic engineering they can — in theory — be relatively easily modified to produce all sorts of useful proteins, compared with the effort required to modify a plant or animal.

Most of the earliest commercial applications of biotechnology have been in the production of pharmaceutical proteins, such as human interferon and growth hormone. The relevant human genes have been engineered into a bacterium or yeast, followed by its large-scale culture and the extraction and purification of the mass-produced protein product.

Bacterial cultures are easier to handle than those of other cells. They are 1,000 times simpler genetically than plant or animal cells, and grow 70-80 times faster. Bacteria divide every 30 minutes on average; plant cells in tissue culture typically take two weeks to double their numbers.

Tropical developing countries abound with useful microbes and fungi in soils and in rainforests. They represent a resource to be exploited, if only the research could be more solidly established. But the world of bacteria and microscopic fungi is vast and little explored; and few microbes have yet been sufficiently researched at a molecular level for useful genetic improvements or transfers to be made.

Nevertheless, potential developments include:

- Agricultural uses of microbes that grow naturally and harmlessly on plant leaves or roots. Modified bacteria could kill insect pests, act as natural nitrogen fertiliser, or prevent frost damage. The market for agriculturally useful microbes is predicted to reach US$1 billion annually by the year 2000 [1].

Bacterial protein factories

The first commercial application of genetic engineering was the creation of transgenic bacteria, designed as "protein factories" for the mass-production of valuable proteins for commercial and research purposes.

Bacteria engineered to carry and express genes from humans, animals and viruses, mostly directed at the lucrative health markets of richer countries, are now producing human factor VIII (for haemophiliacs), human insulin (for diabetics), human interferons, human growth hormone (for growth-retarded children), hormones such as erythropoietin (which stimulates red blood cell formation and is needed by patients with faulty kidneys), tissue plasminogen activator (to prevent thrombosis), and virus proteins (for use in vaccines).

These proteins can otherwise only be obtained from human cadaver tissue, or occur in such small amounts that they are impossible to purify in sufficient quantities. Factor VIII used to be partially purified from human blood plasma, and in recent years many haemophiliacs were infected with HIV (the virus that causes AIDS) by this route. Making viral proteins in this way is also safer than growing large amounts of live infectious virus.

- Improving or extending the range of microbes used in traditional fermentations of foods and drinks.

- Making "single-cell protein" for animal and human food.

- Making industrial chemicals such as biodegradable plastics.

- Extracting minerals — particularly copper — from low-grade deposits.

- Selecting and improving microbes to make useful products from wastes, to reduce pollution and to clean water.

- Exploiting micro-algae (single-celled aquatic green plants).

- Exploiting fungi.

PEST-KILLING MICROBES

One of the most practicable applications may be bacteria which have been selected, or modified, to kill insect pests.

The insect-killing toxin genes of the bacterium *Bacillus thuringiensis*, often found in diseased insects or in soil or plant debris, have already been successfully transferred to some plants, to protect them against insect attack (see Chapter 4). The genes produce the toxins (poisons) in the form of crystalline proteins.

But the un-engineered bacteria themselves — and the related *Bacillus sphaericus* — are already being widely used as sprays to kill pests in forestry and agriculture. They are also used to kill the larvae of blackflies, the vectors of river blindness, in the World Health Organization's West African Onchocerciasis Control Programme (OCP).

The advantages of the bacteria as pesticides include:

- High specificity of strains to particular insects, allowing close targeting of what insects are killed (some insects are helpful predators of pests, and should be left alive).

- Insects lack good resistance mechanisms to the bacterial toxins, according to present evidence, compared with the resistance that can develop to chemical insecticides. For example, resistance to insecticides has been a serious matter for the OCP.

- Reduction in the need for applications of environmentally dangerous chemical pesticides.

- Biodegradability — although too-rapid biodegradation, before the bacterial toxins have had their full effect on the insects, is a disadvantage of this toxin which is rather sensitive to sunlight.

- Non-toxicity to humans and animals — although these claims have to be confirmed for each new variety of toxin developed.

- Cheapness and simplicity of production in bacterial culture, so that sprays can be made locally. Up to one-third of the dry weight of the cultured bacteria can be pure crystalline toxin.

Kunthala Jayaraman and colleagues at Anna University, Madras, India, are capitalising on these advantages and are studying the molecular genetics of *Bacillus sphaericus*, aiming at the control of malarial mosquitoes [2]. They want to select strains that: are highly potent against mosquito larvae; survive at the relatively high Indian ambient temperatures, and persist in the water where the larvae grow; and are easy to cultivate, extract and distribute, using cheap natural resources.

Some *B. sphaericus* strains have proved very effective against mosquitoes in trials around Madras and Madurai, claim Jayaraman and colleagues, and have remained active for some 40 days. Other researchers are working on bacterial strains carrying genes that kill rice pests such as the brown plant-hopper, a vector of rice tungro virus.

Study of the precise molecular action of the toxins on the insects will also help in strain selection. Eventually it may be possible to "design" toxins to attack specific insects and engineer these artificial genes into selected bacteria.

One disadvantage of the bacteria is that they do not naturally colonise plants, so regular re-spraying is necessary. The US Monsanto Corporation has transferred the *B. thuringiensis* toxin genes to a bacterium that does colonise plants — *Pseudomonas fluorescens*, which lives around maize roots. The bacterial strain so far developed is not very good at killing the main US root pest, corn rootworm, but more research to select a better toxin gene should improve it.

A difficulty with the bacteria at present sprayed in West Africa against blackflies is that they sink rapidly in water, so their effectiveness in killing surface-breathing insect larvae is short-lived — they biodegrade too rapidly. Work is now going on to select strains that will float, and so be more effective. In India, the toxin genes are being introduced into blue-green algae, which do float.

Other insecticidal proteins include *chitinases* — enzymes that attack and destroy chitin, the main component of the hard body-parts of insects. These are produced by several bacteria of the genera *Serratia*, *Streptomyces*, and *Vibrio*, and by fungi. Work is afoot to clone the genes into plant-colonising *Pseudomonas* [3].

Some work has been done on controlling locusts with fungal chitinases which specifically attack locusts and grasshoppers. These would be formulated and sprayed just like existing pesticides, would be biodegradable, and would be advantageous if they proved cheaper, more effective and less environmentally harmful than other pesticides. They could be available and approved by 1995-2000, according to locust specialist Joyce Major of the UK Overseas Development Natural Resources Institute.

Genetic manipulation of fungi pathogenic to insects has been "talked about", but real research progress on control methods will probably only follow a better biological understanding of the insects' complex behaviour, according to Major.

MICROBES FOR NITROGEN FERTILISER

Useful microbes abound in plant root systems: in particular the bacteria *Rhizobium* and *Bradyrhizobium* which colonise the roots of leguminous plants and trees, forming nitrogen-fixing "nodules". Other nitrogen-fixing bacteria relatives are *Frankia*, which grow in the roots of alder trees. All these species make natural fertiliser by "fixing" atmospheric nitrogen into a form easily assimilated by the plant. Some free-living microbes, such as *Klebsiella* and many blue-green algae, also fix nitrogen. All are possible targets of biotechnologists.

The techniques of adding nitrogen-fixing bacteria to soil and seedlings are known as *inoculation*. Rhizobium cultures are already produced and sold as substitutes for nitrogen fertilisers. They are added to the soil when seeds are planted. They would be much more widely used if biotechnology could make them more effective, especially if they could be made to fix nitrogen for other types of plants [4].

In sub-Saharan Africa for example, some improved high-yielding maize varieties have failed under field conditions because they require more inputs such as fertiliser than poor farmers can give. A self-sustaining maize plant that can make its own fertiliser was one long-term goal identified by African scientists at a meeting in Yamoussoukro, Côte d'Ivoire, in 1989.

Much investment in the study of nitrogen-fixing genes and the biochemistry of these microbes has not yet, however, yielded any great practical advances. The system is extremely complicated. It involves numerous so-called *nif* (nitrogen-fixing) genes in the bacteria (17 in *Klebsiella*), and genes in the plant. The nitrogen-fixing system is very sensitive to oxygen, so that reactions must go on in specialised, tightly sealed tissues such as the nodules on legume roots.

Reducing fertiliser imports and use by making plants such as rice or maize fix their own nitrogen is attractive. But most experts feel it is still in the realm of science fiction. Neither direct nif gene transfer into plants, nor adjusting bacterial genes to enable the bacteria to colonise cereals or other plants, seem possible in the short or even medium term.

Scientists are having a little more success with conventional ways of improving nitrogen fixation. They are selecting combinations of plant and bacterial strains that produce the highest crop yield in research plots, and are developing ways of growing plants and bacteria locally, and successfully "inoculating" soil and seedlings.

Inoculation technology is already available for adaptation in many Third World countries, because of the widespread cultivation of soybean, which is dependent on one nitrogen-fixing bacterium — *Bradyrhizobium japonicum*. This bug is not found naturally except in China; elsewhere, it must be inoculated artificially into the soil.

A big problem with inoculants, however, is that the introduced bacteria must compete for a place on the plant with other, less useful but better-adapted strains already in the soil. Often the inoculant cells must outnumber the indigenous ones 1,000:1 before they will take hold, which makes the process less cost-effective by demanding large doses of inoculant.

Nevertheless, Appropriate Technology International, for example, has developed an improved *Rhizobium* strain for soybean farmers in Thailand, and the government has constructed a large-scale fermentation plant to produce it [5]. Thus far, only minor increases in productivity have been obtained. Greater success may come through large-scale screening of natural tropical varieties of nitrogen-fixing soil micro-organisms, which is being organised through the UNESCO/UNEP Microbiological Research Centre Network (MIRCEN).

MICROBES TO PREVENT FROST DAMAGE

Frost damage can be a problem in some developing country regions — such as Northern Asia, and the uplands of Africa and Latin America. Biotechnology offers a solution in the form of *Pseudomonas* bacteria. Up to a million of these harmless bacteria are found per square centimetre of plant surface. In the United States, *Pseudomonas* has already been genetically engineered to reduce frost damage on strawberries.

In this case, the trick was to **remove** a gene, called simply "ice", which normally produces a protein which makes freezing water vapour crystallise to form frost. In experiments, these modified, so-called "ice-minus" bacteria were sprayed onto the strawberry plants to replace the indigenous "ice-plus" bacteria — with the result that the plants were protected from mild frosts.

The experiments, which took place in California, attracted notoriety for being one of the first-ever planned releases of genetically

Strawberries —
spraying "ice-minus"
bacteria protects the
plants from mild
frosts. /*Primrose
Peacock/Holt Studios*

engineered organisms. Public fears of unforeseen consequences delayed the experiments for several years. When they did eventually go ahead, tests showed that the bacteria did not escape from the experimental plots [6].

MICROBES FOR FERMENTATION

Fermented foods — foods in which a micro-organism is deliberately grown — are traditional in many Third World countries, particularly in Asia. Controlled fermentation helps to preserve food, and often increases nutritive value, usually by increasing protein content. Microbiologists hope to improve these processes to adapt them to changing consumer tastes in the cities, and to apply them to producing new foods. This could ensure a continuing cash income for rural food industries [7].

The many micro-organisms responsible for fermentations — yeasts, fungi and bacteria — can be genetically engineered, or scientifically selected, to improve the efficiency, speed and cost of fermentation conversion .

The commercial fermentation processes for making alcohol, citric acid, lactic acid, monosodium glutamate, lysine, xanthan, penicillin and riboflavin, are already much improved and near theoretical limits. But the more complex biological processes for making the amino acid tryptophan (used in animal feeds), some vitamins (including vitamin B12), and some antibiotics, are still inefficient, and costs will be substantially reduced by judicious genetic engineering [8].

Small-scale local agricultural fermentation industries could be developed in Africa to add value to crops, according to the Food and Agriculture Organization (FAO). FAO has fermented food projects in Nigeria and Cameroon. Extensive technical exchange with Asia, where fermented foods — and research into them — are more widespread, would be useful, it says.

Thai researchers have isolated 80 different sorts of yeast from 29 kinds of fermented foods based on fish, shrimp, meat, cereals, and fruit. It seems the fermentation of many foods — such as cheese, sake, soy sauce, and miso — depends on more than one type of micro-organism.

In Indonesia, highly nutritious and digestible tempehs are fermented from soybeans (*kedele*), groundnuts (*ontjom*) and coconuts (*bongkrek*), mostly with *Rhizopus* moulds, increasing protein content by 10-12%. Research is improving the manufacturing process and finding ways of eliminating microbial contaminations (which can produce highly dangerous aflatoxins).

American researchers have adapted tempeh-making techniques to cereals and cassava. Fermentation has increased the protein content of wheat preparations six- or seven-fold, riboflavin content five-fold, and has doubled niacin content.

French research has aimed at using microbes to transform starch-rich foods — such as cassava — into protein-rich ones. Cassava has been transformed from 2-3% protein and 80-90% starch into a food with 18-20% protein and 30-35% carbohydrate after 24-30 hours' fermentation with the mould, *Aspergillus niger*. Cassava has also been treated with *lactobacillus*, which produces a weak acid, lactic acid, to improve its storability.

In Martinique, work has been done on converting waste bananas into animal feed by increasing protein content by fermentation.

Cocoa manufacture also involves fermentation. The beans are mashed and allowed to ferment naturally to develop their flavour before drying and roasting. Yeasts turn pulp sugars into alcohol, then bacteria produce lactic and acetic acids. The temperature of the fermentation reaches as high as 50°C, killing the cocoa seed embryos and releasing enzymes that develop the flavour of cocoa — which depends on some 300 compounds. Work could be done on the microbial populations involved, to improve efficiencies and flavours, but so far little has been attempted.

SINGLE-CELL PROTEIN

Single-cell protein (SCP) — yeasts or bacteria cultured to produce human or animal food or food additives — was a 1960s answer to the predicted food crisis of the 1980s. Mostly using hydrocarbons as food for the microbes, the technology became uneconomic when oil prices rose and world food production remained high. However, SCP is still being produced, particularly in Cuba, using waste molasses from sugar production, and in oil-rich states. Work is also being done on cultivating nutritious yeast from cassava, but 7 kg of cassava make only 1 kg of yeast.

The great dream is that more, rather than less, food could be produced with microbes: 2 kg of yeast can theoretically make 80 tonnes of protein in two months. A broiler chicken — considered the most profitable animal to raise — produces only 2 kg of meat in two months, while **consuming** 8.4 kg of plant protein. Biotechnologists working with SCP will continue working to try to turn this dream into reality [9].

The potential of SCP has been taken seriously in Nigeria, the most populous country in Africa. Nigeria faces a growth in food demand of 3.5% a year. But Nigerians, on average, already consume 20-25% less protein than World Health Organization recommended levels. Some revolution in food production has to take place if Nigerians are not to starve.

A report prepared for the International Labour Office by Gilbert Okereke suggests that single-cell protein could be part of the answer [10]. Nigerian protein demand has been met in part by an expansion of poultry-farming, he says. Yet poultry farmers are currently working at around 50% of production capacity: they need better quality feed — the government has banned foreign soybean and fish meal imports to save foreign exchange — and lower feed prices. SCP could provide that chicken-feed, Okereke believes.

SCP is basically a mass of nutritious micro-organisms, usually fungi, fermented on some cheap organic substance. This was originally oil or gas, until their prices rose too high, forcing early SCP producers out of the market. Nigeria and other countries could grow SCP on agricultural plant wastes, Okereke believes. Waste natural gas — Nigeria flares US$5 million of gas a day from its oilfields — could also be used.

Biotechnology is needed to select and improve organisms to grow on the appropriate available wastes as different organisms may be needed for different wastes. It can also help to develop fermentation processes, and to match the resulting SCP to market requirements in Nigeria.

Market economists must study the costs of collection of the widely scattered wastes, of fermentation and of distribution of the product — which will, first, determine whether the proposal will work at all; and second, determine the optimum scale of fermenter, whether village, urban, regional or national.

The economics of a Nigerian SCP programme would be totally different, however, from those of the failed industrial-world systems, as the organic base and the market are different. Nigeria could base any SCP developments on highly labour-intensive fermentation processes to provide employment.

BUGS FOR THE CHEMICAL INDUSTRY

Microbes have long been used to produce chemicals such as antibiotics — which are the natural weapons of war between one microbe and another — and, of course, alcohol, and the carbon dioxide bubbles that make bread rise.

But now that microbes can be genetically modified, more exotic ideas are afoot, such as engineering bacteria to make plastic.

A cotton ginnery, Tanzania. Cotton will almost certainly be engineered to suit the interests of wealthy Northern producers, unless donors support research appropriate to conditions and pests of developing countries. */Neil Cooper/Euro Action Acord/Panos Pictures*

Bacterial plastics

At present, plastics are made mostly from mineral oil through chemical operations on the oil's hydrocarbon molecules to link them into long chains (a process called polymerisation). A tangle of these long chains, or polymers, is plastic; different chains and different linkages among them make different plastics.

Could microbes do this? Yes. After all, it was the geological degradation of microbes and other life-forms that made mineral oil in the first place. But the real reason for the recent explosion of scientific and industrial interest in biopolymers was the discovery and cloning in the United States in 1988 of the polymer-making genes of a species of Alcaligenes bacteria. The microbes swell to make 80% of their dry weight in the form of a biopolymer called polyhydroxybutyrate

(PHB), apparently as an energy store, when they are threatened by a reduction in their nitrogen supply.

Now, Japan alone has invested US$200 million in biopolymer projects; and ICI, Britain's largest chemical company, is already using vats of *Alcaligenes eutrophus* to produce PHB to make bottles for soft drinks.

In principle, biopolymers like PHB could also be made by plants, and some scientists have talked of the age of the "plastic potato". Microbes, however, can be more easily manipulated, and can be grown under industrial conditions. They will probably be the first source of practical products [11].

Why the interest? Three reasons:

- The biopolymers so far produced are biodegradable — natural microbes will digest them, so bioplastics will be environmentally friendly.

- Biopolymers are a renewable resource, whereas oil will one day run out. In the United States, one of the main funders of biopolymer research has been the Office of Naval Research, because of the strategic need for an indigenous source of plastics, if oil were unavailable.

- The power of the complex chemical processing apparatus of the cell, harnessed by molecular biology, could lead to a revolution in the variety and properties of plastics that could be made.

One day there could be biologically active bioplastics used for cleaning cloths that digest the dirt, for example, or as the basis of replacement organs in the body.

But artificial fibres much closer to natural fibres might also emerge from polymer research, possibly threatening producers of natural fibres like cotton.

Apart from technical obstacles, the main trouble with biopolymers at present is cost: ICI's PHB, at current production rates of just 50 tonnes a year, costs around **30 times as much** as ordinary plastics. But these prices will certainly come down as markets grow, and as production and extraction techniques improve. Nevertheless, for some time, bioplastics will have to sell for a premium, won over perhaps by their environmental credentials.

Ethanol

Ethanol (common alcohol) is another chemical produced from microbes.

Filling up with alcohol mixture in Brazil. /*David Hall/Panos Pictures*

Brazil's cars run on microbes. Yeasts make ethanol as a petrol substitute by fermenting specially grown sugar-cane. Unfortunately, the process is uneconomic and has had to be highly subsidised: as a source of energy, ethanol at around US$34 per barrel of oil equivalent has proved more expensive than oil itself. Furthermore, smallholders have been pushed off the land to grow sugar-cane, which has displaced food crops. Effluent from the distilleries is also causing ecological damage.

Research is under way to increase fermentation efficiency and speed, to decrease fermentation costs. There have also been attempts to develop integrated small-scale distilleries, employing smallholders who also grow the crop.

The Brazilian Government recently banned the construction of new alcohol plants. Nevertheless, Thai researchers are investigating the fermentation of cassava starch to alcohol, after the European Community (EC) closed Europe to cassava imports. In such special circumstances the process could be economic [12].

EXTRACTING MINERALS

B acteria have evolved to tolerate and exploit the most extreme conditions on Earth, from boiling mud-pools around volcanoes to dark, sulphurous under-ocean vents and Antarctic snows.

So perhaps it is not so surprising that some 10-20% of the world copper supply is currently extracted by the use of microbes on poor quality ores and slag heaps. Bugs like *Thiobacillus ferroxidans* enjoy the acid conditions of the spoil heaps of worked-out mines, getting their energy from "burning" or "oxidising" sulphur or iron, and in the process extracting copper. *Thiobacillus ferroxidans* has also been genetically engineered to improve its efficiency in extracting gold from arsenical ores [13].

Further progress is limited by a lack of scientific knowledge of exactly what other bacteria are involved and how they do their work. The extraction process itself is limited by the need for intimate mixing between the ore and the microbes.

But with research, there is little reason to suppose that the techniques could not be extended to other ores in other conditions. Almost certainly there are already micro-organisms, growing in mine conditions throughout the world, that could be exploited to extract small amounts of expensive minerals; they only need to be discovered and brought into use.

BUGS FOR WASTES AND WATER

T he first bacterium to be patented, by Canadian biologist A.M. Chakrabarty, was designed to destroy waste.

His bacterium, selected from several that he found could grow on crude oil, was deliberately stuffed with small circles of bacterial DNA (plasmids) that contained genes whose enzyme products directed the digestion of several oil chemicals. The bug was to be thrown on oil slicks after oil disasters to digest the oil.

Unfortunately, the bug did not digest the most environmentally damaging, large-molecule components of the oil, and it was not successful.

The cleaning of poisonous industrial waste tips by microbes is likely to be even more challenging. But bacteria are already being used to digest domestic sewage and agricultural wastes, and these uses will be extended by biotechnology.

For example, biotechnology is being applied to the selection of heat-loving microbes for composting agricultural wastes into useful manures; and for producing biogas (methane) from the same wastes.

Biotechnology promises major improvements to such intermediate technologies. In one simple experiment, for example, researchers found that methane-producing bacteria are greatly assisted by the addition of a few hydrogen-producing bacteria.

However, rural biogas production in developing countries is probably less limited by the precise microbiology involved than by the capital cost of the concrete and tanks required, by the need for maintenance, and by the availability of wastes (only "two-cow families" can provide enough).

In the Malaysian oil palm industry, however, where up to three cubic metres of highly polluting waste are generated for every tonne of oil, plantation owners have established commercial fermentation systems to make methane from the wastes. The methane is then fed to on-site, energy-intensive industries, while the residue is used as fertiliser for the palms. The palm oil wastes have also been used to make single-cell protein.

Research is also being done on cleaning polluted water with microbes — but as with industrial waste, the problem is to arrange for the degradation of a large variety of pollutants, which will require a complex series of reactions and many different genes.

EXPLOITING MICRO-ALGAE

Micro-algae — microscopic plants that get their energy from sunlight by photosynthesis — are used for producing animal and fish food and purifying waste water. They could also be grown as sources of chemicals and biochemicals, such as polyunsaturated fatty acids (useful food-stuffs which are rare in plant and animal sources). Blue-green algae (which are not plants at all, but a type of photosynthetic bacteria) are also a source of nitrogen fertiliser, as they

Blue-green algae in India

The Indian Agricultural Research Institute (IARI) can supply starter cultures of nitrogen-fixing blue-green algae for rice farmers quite cheaply — at 25 US cents per packet. But IARI has problems, familiar to many laboratories, in getting its products known and widely distributed. These problems could well be exacerbated by the advent on the scene of Seed Technologies, a US firm based in Iowa, which is hoping to capture the blue-green algae market in India by manufacturing its own brand of culture locally.

Despite the higher price (US$15 a packet) and sophistication (it needs a sprayer), it can potentially displace the IARI product because of high-pressure salesmanship, says Dr G.S. Venkataraman, Research Director of IARI, and who initiated blue-green algae technology in India. "If a poor farmer has to pay $15 to import blue-green algae I will give up my research," he says. "Why should I work if my product does not reach our farmers?"

Nitrogen-fixing blue-green algae occur naturally in a flooded paddy field in Bengal. Biotechnology could improve the strains of algae. /*Paul Harrison/Panos Pictures*

Nitrogen-fixing blue-green algae occur naturally in a flooded paddy field in Bengal. Biotechnology could improve the strains of algae. /Paul Harrison/Panos Pictures

can fix atmospheric nitrogen into a form usable by plants.

The requirements for growing algae, shallow water, sunlight and relatively cheap nutrients, are unsophisticated. The US biotechnology company Cyanotech is planning to use blue-green algae to produce beta-carotene, a vitamin A precursor, at a fraction of normal cost.

The micro-alga *Botryococcus braunii* produces a kind of vegetable oil: it contains 20% hydrocarbons during its fastest phase of growth. FAO is considering an experiment to grow it to produce oil on Lake Chad in Central Africa. Around Lake Chad, villagers have traditionally eaten another micro-alga — the protein-rich *Spirulina* — with their cereal meals. In Chad it is considered a good substitute for meat sauce.

Bengali rice cultivators have long exploited nitrogen-fixing blue-green algae which occur naturally in the flooded paddy fields. Rice yields can reach 4 tonnes per hectare without any application of chemical fertilisers or manure. The appropriate application of biotechnology here might be to enhance the effectiveness of such existing techniques, rather than implanting completely novel ones.

The Bangladesh Rice Research Institute is already seeking improved strains of blue-green algae. The Indian Agricultural Research Institute (IARI) in New Delhi supplies blue-green algae starter cultures which small farmers can multiply and spread on their rice fields; it has a collection of more than 400 strains to suit different conditions. Israeli scientists at the Algal Biotechnology Research Laboratory are selecting and developing strains to suit different ecological zones.

Commercially, micro-algae are produced in the South mostly as health food for the North, as production costs are high; but research could decrease costs and make algae more widely available as a food in the Third World. Current industrial yields of 10-30 tonnes of dry weight per hectare per year could be increased to 70 tonnes; the theoretical maximum (limited by the efficiency of photosynthesis) is 200 tonnes.

ENGINEERING FUNGI

Like bacteria, fungi are everywhere. Some are eaten; some cause billions of dollars of damage to crops; others cause human disease; some are cultured in industry to make the key antibiotics, penicillin and cephalosporin. Biotechnology could therefore have great impact, if benign fungi could be engineered to be more useful and productive, or the harmful ones understood so well that they could be better diagnosed or destroyed.

Fungi exist by scavenging from other life-forms, dead or alive. They can be single-celled like the yeast, *Saccharomyces cerevisiae* (brewers' or bakers' yeast), or multi-celled, threadlike "filamentous" fungi.

S. cerevisiae has been the target of genetic engineers because its cells are very much more like those of plants and animals than are bacteria. That means it can handle the protein products of introduced human, plant or animal genes more faithfully than can bacterial cells, and also have the advantage of rapid multiplication and easy mass production.

Yeast is already being used commercially as a "host" for the gene for a hepatitis B virus protein. This protein is mass-produced to make an effective vaccine against hepatitis B.

Equally interesting are the filamentous fungi, which are those most familiar to us as moulds, mushrooms and toadstools. They grow as a succession of single cells strung together to make fine threads, or filaments, which make the fluffy mass seen on mouldy bread, for instance. Mushrooms and toadstools, or the tiny blue or black specks on bread moulds, are the fruiting bodies of the fungus, which produce spores.

Almost all plants need fungi to grow. Plant roots are usually entangled with fungi in symbiotic structures called mycorrhiza; these help the plants extract nutrients from the soil. It may one day be possible to improve the effectiveness of mycorrhiza to enable crops to survive in harsher conditions on less nutrients.

Other filamentous fungi attack plants, rather than help them, causing enormous damage to crops. With more research on the molecular mechanisms of economically important, plant-pathogenic fungi, it should be possible to design diagnostic probes. In the long term, new types of treatment or protective strategies may be developed against plant-pathogenic fungi.

So far, work is progressing slowly as fungi are much more complicated than viruses. Conventional fungicides are often effective but expensive. In-built resistance to fungal disease could be of great benefit to developing country crops.

CHAPTER 9

ANIMAL, FISH AND INSECT BIOTECHNOLOGY

There is considerable scope for improving animal productivity in developing countries. These countries have 74% of the world's population, produce 50% of the world's plant resources — but only 25% of the animal resources. Average meat consumption in the South is 13 kg per head per year, compared with 75 kg in the developed world. But in the South, animals are used for more than food: in India, 60% of draught power is provided by cattle.

Disease destroys some 35% of current developing country animal production, including milk and eggs. This is double the proportion lost in the industrialised world. Hides and skins are by-products of meat production, but developing country hides are generally poor. Ticks and diseases cause blemishes which greatly reduce their value. Global figures for economic losses caused by animal diseases put foot and mouth at the top (US$50 billion annually), followed by mastitis ($35 billion), Rift Valley Fever ($7.5 billion), and leptospirosis ($4.5 billion). But these figures almost certainly underestimate rural losses in developing countries, many of which do not appear in economic statistics [1].

Six main biotechnologies have emerged in animal production and health:

- Genetic engineering of animals. As in plant breeding, selected genes can be transferred into some animal species, to introduce new and useful genetic traits.

- Embryo technology. Cattle and sheep breeding can be accelerated by multiple ovulation and embryo transfer.

- Disease diagnosis. Molecular probes, such as monoclonal antibodies and DNA probes (see Chapter 4), can be used to diagnose disease and make accurate studies of its distribution and spread.

- New vaccines. Genetically engineered vaccines (see Chapter 6) against animal diseases are being developed.

- Gene mapping. As in plant breeding, accurate genetic maps can help to locate and isolate desirable genes.

- The use of growth hormones, mass-produced from cloned genes, to increase the rate of growth and milk production.

The prospects for embryo transfer, disease probes, vaccines and gene maps for the developing world are reasonable; but the production of transgenic animals is extremely expensive and beyond the reach of most developing countries.

The International Livestock Centre for Africa (ILCA) in Addis Ababa anticipates useful advances in livestock production for developing countries from growth hormones and new vaccines and antibiotics. It also envisages the possibility of genetic alteration of the micro-organisms in the stomachs (rumen) of cattle and other cud-chewing animals. Rumen bacteria might, for example, be engineered to produce growth hormones, delivered direct to the animal. Genetic engineering may also be able to transfer resistance to trypanosomiasis from wild to domestic livestock [2].

GENETIC ENGINEERING

Genes from almost any source can now be introduced into animal species, notably laboratory mice and rats, some domesticated animals, and some insects and fish.

But the efficiency of genetic engineering in animals has so far been low. In mice, for example, only around 4% of treated eggs result in a genetically modified animal which can transmit the introduced gene — the transgene — to the next generation.

The costs of genetic engineering experiments with large animals like cattle are enormous. A recent example, in which three sheep were raised in Scotland with introduced genes so that they would produce human blood clotting factors in the milk, is said to have cost some US$2 million. When refined, however, gene transfer may enable the production of animals with faster growth, longer wool, or resistance to specific diseases [3].

In the North, the idea of producing genetically engineered cattle which produce valuable human pharmaceuticals in their milk, which can then be extracted, is being actively canvassed. The experimental sheep are an early stage in such developments.

A FEW BASICS... transgenic animals

In most animals, and certainly those of practical interest to genetic engineers, the fertilised egg is the only cell from which a new animal can develop. So if the animal is to carry the transplanted gene in all its cells, it must be introduced into the fertilised egg or the very early embryo (when it consists of only a few cells).

Genetic modifications made to the fertilised egg are carried over to all the cells that arise from it. Because the new gene is therefore present in future reproductive cells, it can also be passed on from one generation to another to breed a stable strain of genetically modified animals.

For mammals, the techniques of in vitro fertilisation, embryo storage and embryo transfer provide the required background for genetic modification of the in vitro fertilised egg.

Mammalian egg cells are quite large and the nucleus can be seen under a high-power optical microscope. DNA can be injected directly into the nucleus using the finest of micropipettes (fine glass tubes). This way it has a much better chance of being stably incorporated into the chromosomes than if it were injected into the cytoplasm and had to find its way across the membrane barrier surrounding the nucleus. The modified fertilised egg is then replaced in the uterus of a receptive female where it implants and develops normally.

Although the individual success rate per egg is low, strains of so-called transgenic mice, pigs, sheep and cows have been bred, carrying a variety of genes from sources ranging from bacteria to humans.

EMBRYO TRANSFER

Embryo transfer increases the number of offspring a cow can have, and even allows individual eggs to be divided in the test-tube to give two identical eggs — which will produce identical twins. This is the nearest equivalent in animals of the tissue culture cloning of elite plants.

To produce embryos, a cow of elite genetic stock is stimulated with drugs to produce many eggs at once (a process called superovulation). Then the eggs are fertilised in vitro with sperm from an elite breeding bull. The fertilised eggs taken from the original mother are then implanted into the womb of "surrogate" mothers, where they will develop normally. The surrogate mother does not need to be of genetically superior stock as she will not make any genetic contribution to her offspring.

The elite cow is therefore not burdened with pregnancy, which prevents ovulation for several months. Without the pregnancy, she will soon ovulate again, and the process can be repeated. Using embryo transfer, selected elite cows can produce 17 calves in their lifetime, compared with the average 3.5.

Since the technology is now relatively routine, the big question is to define what would be a useful elite stock for a given region. For example, some Nigerian scientists do not put the breeding of

Improving Indian cattle

The Indian Department of Biotechnology's "cattle herd improvement programme" aims to double annual milk production from the present 40 million to 80 million tonnes in 10 years.

India has more than 250 million cattle and 70 million buffaloes, most of them poor yielders and an economic burden. These will be used as surrogate mothers to produce elite calves. A combination of embryo transfer technology and "Talsur" — a new vaccine to sterilise unwanted bulls — is India's strategy to replace inferior cattle with elite breeds.

Beginning in 1992, 10,000 calves will be born every year by embryo transfer, the department claims.

The programme, co-ordinated by the National Dairy Development Board, aims to produce a seed stock of 2,500 bulls and bull mothers using one main laboratory, four regional centres and one or more centres in each of the 22 states.

The main laboratory (at Bidaj in Gujarat) and the regional centres (in Uttar Pradesh, Andhra Pradesh and Maharastra), and the state centre (at Erode in Tamil Nadu) are already operational. "A farmer simply has to bring his cow or buffalo to one of the centres and collect it after the embryo transfer," says the department secretary, Dr S. Ramachandran. The service will cost a farmer US$130 (mostly for hormones), but should triple his income.

The reproductive technology developed in India in the last two years include superovulation, to get 30 or more eggs from elite donor cows at a time, in vitro fertilisation, and twinning by splitting the fertilised egg in vitro before replacement in the surrogate mother. The embryo technology project has so far resulted in the birth of 75 elite calves, 13 of them from buffaloes.

trypanosomiasis-resistant cattle as a high priority, as it would be almost impossible to ensure that they would be universally adopted by largely nomadic herdsmen; and in a herd containing even a few non-resistant cattle, the genetic resistance could soon be diluted and lost by interbreeding. They believe that efforts to control the tsetse fly itself could be more rewarding.

Induced twinning, used simply to produce more of the same, is in the opinion of some African scientists of more use to African herdsmen than the idea of breeding super-cattle of higher quality, which might require higher quality inputs and more care.

Even so, a successful embryo transfer programme will require a highly experienced staff, and high capital investment for facilities, equipment and drugs to induce superovulation. At present, such work takes place almost exclusively in the developed world, and the elite stocks used are rarely appropriate for Third World conditions.

DISEASE PROBES

The successful control of disease requires accurate and rapid diagnosis and this is where biotechnology has made most difference. Highly specific monoclonal antibodies or sensitive DNA probes can be made which will react with a specific disease organism. In addition, monoclonals can be made to detect the antibodies induced by a particular disease in an animal — which is sometimes the best way of detecting whether an animal has been infected.

For the field-worker, the test chemicals are provided precoated on small glass or plastic plates. Blood or other samples are dabbed on the plates, and washed off with a simple reagent. Typically, a colour change indicates the presence of the disease. Many such tests are already available. For example, Pirbright Laboratory in the United Kingdom is supplying African countries with test kits for rinderpest virus.

DNA probes are the more specific of the two test systems: they can be used to distinguish previously clinically indistinguishable ailments, such as infections caused by rinderpest on the one hand, and the "peste des petits ruminants" virus (PPRV) on the other. Such tests are important in tracing the origin of, and thus controlling, a disease outbreak, like the recent rinderpest outbreak in Sri Lanka.

ANIMAL VACCINES

Genetically engineered vaccines have been developed for scours, a neonatal diarrhoea of cattle and pigs; foot and mouth, a cattle disease endemic in South America, Asia and Africa as well as Europe; rabies; and pseudorabies, a herpes virus which attacks the nerve cells of pigs, causing Aujesky's disease. The pseudorabies vaccine consists of the live virus disabled by genetic engineering: it has one critical gene deleted [4].

An Ethiopian scientist is developing an engineered vaccine against rinderpest. Synthetic peptide vaccines are under development against foot and mouth virus. Other types of novel vaccines are being investigated against coccidiosis, a major poultry disease.

Among the international laboratories, the International Laboratory for Research on Animal Diseases (ILRAD) in Nairobi is working on East Coast Fever, a cattle disease caused by a number of related parasites transmitted by ticks. Monoclonal antibodies were used to identify a parasite antigen common to all the parasite varieties, raising the possibility of developing a vaccine against the disease [5].

GENE MAPPING

Progress in producing genetic maps, which show the location of useful genes on the chromosomes, and can trace the movement of genes in breeding programmes, is faster using recombinant DNA

People of the Kamba tribe work as a co-operative, planting maize in the Kitui district in Kenya. Draught animals have been little-used in Africa, partly because of the ravages of animal trypanosomiasis. The control of tsetse flies, resistant animals, and new drugs or vaccines could help. /*Betty Press/Panos Pictures*

technology, and will help animal breeders to find and transfer the genes for useful traits.

Complete mapping of the much smaller number of genes in viruses has been achieved for most important disease viruses, and is helping to identify genes for use in vaccines.

GROWTH HORMONES

Bovine growth hormone (bovine somatotropin or BST), produced from genetically engineered bacteria, is already in use in the United States for increasing the milk yield of dairy cows.

BST has, however, proved to be an entirely inappropriate use of biotechnology, according to a recent US opinion survey [6]. In the US, it seems that many commentators — the US public and small farmers — see no value in the technology. The US already has a milk surplus, and people are suspicious about the effects of BST in the milk they drink. Its benefits are perceived to be towards reducing the costs of large dairy farmers, which could push smaller farmers out of the market.

INSECT BIOTECHNOLOGY

Quite apart from new methods to control pests through modified bacteria and plants, insect science — entomology — is being shaken by molecular biology and biotechnology no less than any other branch of biology.

In the academic world, the molecular genetics of the growth and development of insects is rapidly becoming clear through work on the tiny fruit-fly, Drosophila.

At a practical level, DNA probes are now being used to distinguish insect species and discover new ones. The beginnings of genetic engineering of insects other than fruit-flies has emerged with work on DNA transfer in honey-bees, using modified honey-bee sperm. The possible goal is insecticide-resistant bees, so that swarms could be easily purified of intruders. However, this raises fears of interbreeding, leading, say, to insecticide- resistant killer bees. As a first step, a team of Texan and Canadian scientists have found genes in a soil bacterium that confer insecticide resistance, and transferred them into Drosophila [7].

Bee-keeper in Thailand. In some areas of the world, honey is an important cash product. Bees may also one day be genetically transformed, as growing numbers of molecular biologists are entering insect science. /*Ron Giling/Panos Pictures*

Insects are not all harmful: spinning silk from silk-worm cocoons using traditional "charka" in this South India home. *ICooper and Hammond/Panos Pictures*

Much of this work has happened in the past few years. Two of the first-ever conferences on molecular insect science were recently held in the US. The organiser, John Law of the University of Arizona, said that three years ago the links between molecular biology and insect science were "crude" — but "now it's cutting-edge molecular biology".

Researchers are abandoning study of higher animals because of pressures from animal rights groups, says Law. Some are moving into plant science, and many are moving into insect science with its millions of species and — until now — little research.

The result will certainly be new and more sophisticated techniques to control and use insects, but as yet the work is in its infancy. The message for developing country researchers and their benefactors is to ensure that insects important to Southern agriculture and health, such as bees (over 40% of the world's 1-million-tonne annual honey production comes from developing countries) and silk caterpillars (important to China, India, South Korea and Brazil), as well as key pests, are included in the burgeoning insect molecular biology research programmes.

AQUATIC BIOTECHNOLOGY

Developing countries also produce about 45% of the world's 85-million-tonne annual fish production. Much more could be produced by properly researched aquaculture, to which biotechnology could contribute.

Tilapia, a small all-season fish eaten by the poor of many countries throughout the Third World, is the target of recombinant-DNA research in India. The goal is to make them bigger. In what is India's first transgenic experiment, scientists are now trying to clone the bovine growth hormone gene and micro-inject it into the fertilised egg of tilapia.

Marine organisms other than fish are a hitherto largely untapped source of useful products. Improved ways of cultivating marine life — from shellfish to algae — combined with biotechnology, aim to extend the range of useful products, such as drugs.

Farming of valuable shellfish such as oysters and abalones is being improved as more of the chemical factors that encourage shellfish larvae to settle and mature into adults are being identified.

Those developing countries with rich marine resources could well benefit from such developments if effective research institutes, or links with research institutes in the North, could be established [8].

FOCUS ON RINDERPEST

On the trail of a rinderpest vaccine

Tilahun Daniels Yilma, born on his family's coffee farm in southern Ethiopia, and now Professor of Veterinary Microbiology and Immunology at the University of California, in the United States, believes he has genetically engineered a virus to make vaccine that will halt the animal disease, rinderpest, which kills 2 million cattle a year world-wide and has even begun to affect sheep and goats in India.

In the 1960s and 1970s, an attempt was made to eliminate rinderpest from Africa with an early vaccine. But the campaign failed, and the disease returned for several reasons: it turned out not to be confined to herded cattle, but was also prevalent among animals in the wild, making it impossible to vaccinate the whole population; reinfection occurred through movement of nomadic herds, and through the disruptions caused by wars; and significantly, since the vaccine required freezing and had to be imported, it was difficult to deliver.

Yilma's vaccine can overcome this last hurdle. It does not need freezing, and can even be made locally.

The vaccine, developed with US$870,000 funding from the US Agency for International Development (USAID), is based on the vaccinia virus which was used to eliminate smallpox in humans. Yilma has engineered this virus to make parts of the rinderpest virus and therefore stimulate a bull, cow or buffalo's immune system to generate resistance to rinderpest itself.

More of the the vaccine can be made locally by "scarifying" or scratching a cow with a sample of the engineered vaccinia, and letting the vaccinia grow in the scratch — which it does without harming the cow. Upwards of 100,000 doses of the vaccine are produced by liquefying the resulting scab. Although there is no doubt that the vaccine creates immunity, further field trials are necessary to determine how long that immunity lasts.

There is, however, controversy about the wisdom of re-releasing vaccinia into the environment, now that smallpox has been eradicated and human immunity to the pox viruses is weak. It could risk once again infecting the human population with smallpox.

At a meeting held in July 1989, the World Health Organization discussed the issue and recommended that Yilma redevelop the vaccine using a safer strain of vaccinia.

This has proved successful, and his new "Weitz" strain vaccine is awaiting clearance from the Animal and Plant Health Inspectorate Service in the United States. Once cleared, he can embark on the next and all-important step to determine its effectiveness by conducting field trials.

Rinderpest — the name comes from the German word for cattle plague — is an ancient disease which used to infect cattle in Europe but is now largely prevalent in Asia, the Middle East and Africa. At present there are severe outbreaks of rinderpest in Ethiopia, Uganda, Kenya, Nigeria and the Middle East.

Dr Tilahun Daniels Yilma at the University of California.

Eradication of the virus is of major economic importance to many countries. Somalia, for example, earns 90% of its foreign exchange through the sale of livestock products. During a rinderpest outbreak, however, these products are embargoed. And with the most virulent strains of rinderpest — of which the Sudanese strain is one — the animal can die within 10-12 days.

Even more worrying, however, is the discovery in the last decade that the virus is transmissible between species — and that it is now affecting sheep and goats in India. This has major implications for the control of rinderpest, because the UN Food and Agriculture Organization estimates that there are more than 100 million sheep and goats in India alone.

Modern transportation and the export of live cattle between countries has also resulted in the disease being introduced into areas not previously affected. Turkey, for example, was free of the disease from 1932 but was re-infected in 1970. In addition, many African countries have difficulties, both economic and political, in maintaining quarantine, monitoring herds and vaccinating young calves.

Such logistical problems and the war between Ethiopia and Somalia over the Ogaden region, stymied previous, intensive vaccination efforts to eradicate rinderpest. Natural and nomadic reservoirs of the virus require vaccines to be supplied continuously to vaccinate young animals. Complete eradication is no longer seen as possible.

The largest effort yet to eliminate rinderpest was the Joint Programme 15 from 1962 to 1976, which attempted the mass vaccination of all cattle in 22 countries from Central to West, East and North-East Africa — covering a total of about 80 million cattle.

The Plowright tissue culture vaccine used in the programme was enormously successful in the early days and achieved significant reductions in the incidence of rinderpest. But by 1982, over 1 million cattle were once again infected. The same approach, using the same vaccine, is now again being tried in the latest fight by the Pan African Rinderpest Campaign.

However, the Plowright vaccine deteriorates in high temperatures and needs to be kept refrigerated. Yilma's vaccine eliminates these problems: hence its exciting promise.

CHAPTER 10

PRIVATE AND PUBLIC BIOTECHNOLOGY

PRIVATE AGRICULTURE, PUBLIC HEALTH

One of the fundamental problems facing biotechnologists working in, or for, developing countries, and the developing countries themselves, is that increasing numbers of useful genes and related expertise are coming under private control: Northern private companies are investing heavily in biotechnology, far outweighing public spending.

There are two options for those working outside those companies. They can either come into conflict, or negotiate to make the best of a weak situation.

At the centre of the issue are profits. Companies may find it easier to make a profit out of Third World agriculture than out of Third World health.

On the whole, major Northern pharmaceutical companies have shown little interest in research and development to improve health in developing countries. The South has been used as a market for surplus products, but the development of new medical products is expensive. The research and development costs of new drugs and vaccines cannot be covered by the poor. Hopes of raising funds for the development of new vaccines are thus centring on public, not private support (see Chapter 6).

In brief, Third World health research has not been thought to pay — except where resulting products will serve rich visitors such as servicemen, businessmen and women or tourists needing short-term protection.

Nevertheless, the US chemical giant Merck has donated the drug ivermectin to the World Health Organization to cure West Africans of river blindness. But that research was already paid for in sales to US farmers for use on animals. In the past, such moves have been largely to do with sales of excess production, or corporate public relations.

The interest of the private sector in agricultural biotechnology in the Third World is to do with making profits as well as projecting

Free drug to halt river blindness

In a fast-flowing river valley in northern Cameroon, as in many such valleys in West Africa, river blindness (onchocerciasis) caused by a microscopic worm carried by blackflies, is rampant.

A villager in the valley is bitten by blackflies 100 times a day — and 95% of the inhabitants of 50 villages in the valley have the disease, which eventually causes blindness when millions of young worms fill a sufferer's eyes. Between 4% and 15% of the people are blind.

Yet this disease could be dramatically reduced by a drug first developed by the US pharmaceutical company, Merck, to eliminate worms from farm animals.

The drug, ivermectin (trade name, Mectizan), kills the young worms that cause blindness and other symptoms, but not the adults from which the young come; it appears that yearly — or even less frequent — retreatment will rid patients of the worst effects of the disease.

And Merck has offered the drug free to the World Health Organization.

The UNDP/World Bank/WHO's Tropical Disease Research Programme is now completing trials in several West African countries — including Cameroon — and in Latin America and Asia, to test its usefulness in the field. First indications are that it offers great hope to millions of sufferers, and that it could help open up valleys — where the larvae of the blackfly vectors abound in fast-flowing, highly oxygenated rivers — to greater rice production and economic farming.

It is a development which — while not strictly one of biotechnology — demonstrates that, in the right circumstances, major Western companies can deliver advanced technologies apparently altruistically to the South.

Merck provides the drug free to any local, national or international onchocerciasis control programme that will meet WHO and national criteria of drug delivery and disease monitoring. Final clinical trials have been under way in Cameroon, Liberia, Malawi, Nigeria and Guatemala.

The key problem to be faced now is how to deliver the drug to those who need it. With delivery costs approaching US$5 per year per patient, few seem likely to receive it unless these costs are underwritten by donors.

Father and child... victims of river blindness in Burkina Faso. /*Paul Harrison/Panos Pictures*

images. Some of their profits will come from plantation crops such as oil palm or cacao; some from total substitutions of one crop, or an industrial process, for another.

However, it is argued, the profit motive does not automatically spell doom for the South. Donald Duvick, the research director of Pioneer Hi-Bred International, the world's largest seed company, says: "I do not think the needs of seed companies for profits are incompatible with their ability to serve the true agricultural needs of the developing countries."

In particular, if a technology could be developed for the South which made a profit there — for example, by improving a cash crop, or developing a new biological resource, or a new process for an old one — that possibility of profit also offers returns for the company, and thus room for negotiations between the user country and the company.

NEGOTIATING GENE DEALS

There is more co-operation and willingness than anyone thinks" on the part of multinational companies to transfer useful technologies to developing countries, according to Roger Beachey of Washington University, St Louis, in the United States. He should know: he is close to one of the big agricultural biotechnology companies, Monsanto, and was himself one of the US biotechnologists who developed the technique of inducing virus resistance in plants by transplanting virus coat-protein genes into them.

"A lot of things are negotiable" with private industry, Beachey claims. Companies might donate technologies in which they would find it difficult to make any profit in developing countries (as Merck donated ivermectin), provided they had guarantees that the technologies could not be passed on or sold to competitors.

Why would companies take such a risk? Certainly to improve their public image, and to avoid their real markets in the industrialised world being threatened by boycotts and other public pressure — just as oil and other companies have attempted to polish their green credentials.

They would also like to improve their image among developing countries, to help the making of profits. If biotechnology takes off in the South, there will be profits to be made in improved cash crops — and companies will smooth their paths by establishing themselves as "good guys" through working on health, food yields and food security.

Companies will also wish to maintain access to developing country genetic resources. If developing countries could control the use of their extensive genetic resources, they would have an important negotiating card.

No doubt with some of these points in mind, Monsanto at least, is considering giving away some of its biotechnology to Africa.

If farmers and scientists can use "Monsanto genes" (ones which Monsanto has patented or otherwise controls) to make crops more profitable in Africa, the company says it will give two-thirds of that profit back to African farmers. Of the remaining one-third, Monsanto will keep half and give the other half to the breeder who breeds the useful seeds containing the Monsanto genes.

The snag is that, in order to be profitable, any such improved crop must have a market: there must be a cash return. Targets must therefore be crops such as cotton or coffee.

Applications of Monsanto genes to mostly non-cash, rural food crops, such as cassava, would therefore seem less likely.

However, Monsanto is prepared to give genes to Kenya to make the country's potatoes virus-resistant. "The company is happy to do that, and go through all the legal work to get approval for the release of the engineered potato, because it is good public relations for the company," says Beachey.

Monsanto may therefore be planning both to make a small profit where it can, and to give genes away to enhance its public image where it is unlikely to make profits.

But whatever the motivation, the offers are significant, as Monsanto has invested huge sums in agricultural gene technology. It aims to collect the most useful gene technologies needed for the identification, transfer and patenting of useful genes into crop plants, and thus become the "IBM" of agricultural biotechnology, controlling and defining the framework of crop science world-wide.

With the advent of biotechnology, Monsanto has not rushed to buy seed companies to control plant breeding and the crops to which its chemicals are applied, as other agrochemical companies have done. Instead, Monsanto has gone "upstream", seeking control of the useful genes and techniques, and aiming to design and sell these to breeders when and how it wishes.

Monsanto can already offer genes — or techniques for finding and introducing genes — for virus resistance and herbicide tolerance, and is working on resistance to fungi and improvements in quality such as better protein, oils and solids content of crops.

At a private meeting in London with representatives of the European Commission, and scientists from Zimbabwe, Kenya and Côte d'Ivoire, Monsanto disclosed its plans to give two-thirds of its

African profits back to farmers.

The scientists agreed that the plan could work, but only if:

- African countries are free to identify their own technology targets, whether yield, security of food supplies, or virus- or insect-resistance. "We want the self-respect of doing it ourselves," they say.

- The new genes are properly investigated and approved in the United States for environmental, farmer and user safety. African countries will not use Monsanto technologies that are not also approved for use in the US.

- Centres for breeding-in the Monsanto genes, using techniques such as tissue culture (growing plants from single cells), genetic engineering, and conventional plant breeding, are established in Africa. Monsanto offered help in training.

And, most essential, all partners must benefit economically, the meeting agreed. That means farmer, nation and Monsanto.

The companies' line thus seems to be, "If you don't damage our real markets, we'll do what you want."

The International Agricultural Research Centres (IARCs) also need to be — and in some cases, already are — involved in such negotiations with multinationals. But they need greater legal expertise to reach equitable deals.

The potential for conflict, or negotiation, is also there among developing countries themselves. The Chinese grip on hybrid rice technology is an example of one developing country which has, for its own profit, restricted access to others. The country at the centre of genetic diversity for coffee, Ethiopia, maintains tight control of its coffee germplasm, limiting possible improvements outside the country. A proper international regime and forum for negotiation on such matters would enhance development.

PATENTS AND OWNERSHIP
OF BIOTECHNOLOGY

A key issue in negotiations must be the ownership of biotechnologies, a matter still in legal evolution in several national and international forums. The open question of the ownership of genetic resources, which are greatest by far in the South, and the need for a system of "farmers' rights" that would recognise the efforts of centuries of indigenous farmers in selecting the best varieties for their needs, is discussed in the next chapter.

Potentially, the owners of genetic resources would be developing countries. But no international agreement has yet been reached on the issue.

Meanwhile, the strongest ownership rights over technologies themselves are patents, which require users of the technology to pay the patent-owner royalties. Patents can now be obtained to cover the construction of novel genes, and even the genes themselves, where sufficiently altered from their natural state.

Companies and others that develop useful biotechnologies — such as modified genes, or old genes in new organisms — aim to patent them to get the most return on their investment. Virtually all current patents pertaining to recombinant DNA technologies are held by scientists, institutions or companies in the North.

The protection offered through various forms of "breeders' rights" in several countries is weaker; for example, it allows "research" on the varieties, through which it would certainly be possible, for example, to breed any modified gene — such as virus resistance gene — into a different plant.

So the pressure is on for patents, limited only by some concern in the North about the ethics of patenting, and so owning, life-forms, particularly animals. The first genetically engineered animal to be patented in 1989 was a strain of transgenic mice carrying human cancer- ausing genes, developed by Harvard University scientists and the US Du Pont Corporation for use in cancer research. Ethical issues will also arise over the project to sequence the human genome, where efforts will be made to patent any useful sequences that are discovered.

For the present, patent protection for biotechnology is strongest in the United States. Political pressure is also greatest there for developing countries to recognise US patents, and private biotechnology is most advanced. US courts have so far given patent protection to:

- Processes used in biotechnology (for example, techniques for creating recombinant DNAs, an essential step in the process of isolating a gene from one source and introducing it into a new host).

- Genetically engineered micro-organisms (for example, bacteria carrying human genes directing the production of medically valuable proteins).

- Genetically engineered plants.

- Genetically engineered animals.

Similar patent systems are emerging in Europe and Japan.

Most patent owners will be private companies in the industrialised world — particularly in the US. Increasing numbers of the developing countries' own biotechnologies might also be patented, by governments or by indigenous private industry.

IARCs could also become patent holders over their own biotechnologies. The purpose of their patents would not be to make profits, since their constitution demands that they distribute their products free to the countries that need them. Rather, the IARC patents would be defensive — aiming to block private companies from capitalising on an IARC technology.

With the exception of the IARCs, patenting could be seen to restrict technology flow to those who could pay royalties, and hence restrict it to marketable applications, principally cash crops. On the other hand, a failure by developing countries to recognise patents (the current position in most countries) could mean that no patented technologies are transferred at all.

Indian researchers say that, even now, they often cannot get the necessary DNA "vectors" — the carrier DNAs into which genes are spliced for gene transfer — from abroad, even from other research laboratories, for use in their own research. These vectors are patented and India has not yet signed the Paris Convention. "We are not going to get them unless we sign the Paris Convention on intellectual property rights," says Dr G. Padmanabhan, of the Indian Institute of Science in Bangalore. "If we ask for a vector, the US laboratories don't even reply."

Because it believes that patents will not be recognised, Pioneer Hi-Bred International says it does not expect to release any genetically engineered seeds to the Third World that will breed true. With true-breeding varieties, farmers can save seed from year to year without any loss of quality.

Automatic loss of quality can be built in if the seeds distributed are *F1 hybrids*. Their advantage to the distributor is that they offer a kind of physical technology protection. Although the hybrid plants grown from the supplied seed are good plants, the seeds of those plants, which might be saved by the farmer for a second crop, do not breed true: they grow into something different and usually inferior.

Patent protection might encourage companies to be more adventurous in releasing technologies without such hybrid protection; but it would still imply somehow collecting royalties from small farmers, which would seem an unlikely prospect. Good seed distribution systems, to distribute new seed every year, thus seem to be likely, as with the Green Revolution crops. Distribution systems exist throughout most of Asia, but hardly at all in Africa.

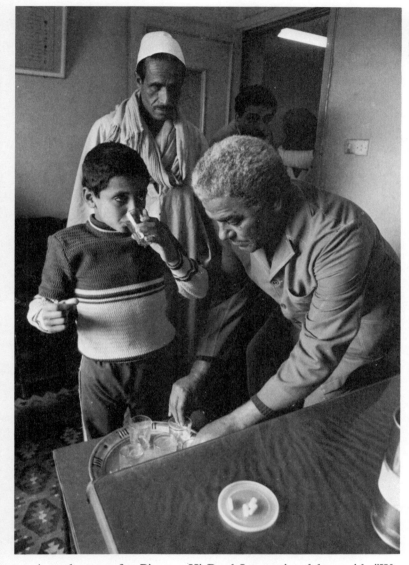

A child in Egypt's Delta region receiving treatment for schistosomiasis. /*Sean Sprague/Panos Pictures*

A spokesman for Pioneer Hi-Bred International has said: "We believe that if there is a patented gene, for example for viral resistance, the breeder that uses that will have to pay royalties." Pioneer was willing to discuss with the IARCs what they needed, said the spokesman. For example, "we could be approached for improved genes for maize without us expecting to make a big profit out of that. Patents don't close those options."

Pioneer adds this warning: "The nature of developing country policies in intellectual property protection will determine whether they are isolated, taken advantage of, or join the world as full partners in the genetic improvement of crop plants."

Privately patented technologies of crops such as sorghum clearly have strong potential in the poorest countries. But private companies would appear to be laying down two conditions: users must recognise the patents, and users must pay royalties (for which they will need aid). It remains to be seen to what exent developing countries will co-operate with these stipulations.

GENES ON THE BLACK MARKET

Suppose that a Northern company put a pesticide gene into oilseed rape for Northern farmers, patented it, and that the variety was available on the market. It would not be too difficult for Southern scientists to extract the gene, and insert it into, say, African cotton — just as Northern scientists have extracted genes from Southern plants and then patented them.

Pioneer Hi-Bred "don't know" how they would react in such circumstances.

There is already a black market in genes. One Pioneer gene has popped up in six different non-company publications, the company says. When people meet at conferences, they don't just exchange ideas — they also exchange tubes and flasks of genes. With powerful biochemical techniques, such as polymerase chain reaction, DNA samples can be multiplied up to useful amounts in a day. However, genes have precise signatures — their exact sequence of bases. Pioneer plans to mark its genes with simple errors that don't affect the gene's workings, and therefore believes it will be able to trace its pirated genes and demand compensation.

Rather than steal a gene, it would better, Pioneer claims, to come and make a deal. Patents are intended to ensure profits; in countries where a patented gene is likely to make no profit, the gene may be given free.

US PUSHES PRIVATE BIOTECHNOLOGY

The US Agency for International Development (USAID) could become a major actor in biotechnology transfer to developing countries. Its interests focus sharply on the private sector, both in fostering collaboration between US private biotechnology companies and developing country researchers (under patent protection), and in encouraging the indigenous commercialisation of biotechnology.

At a USAID meeting on these issues in 1988 [1], participants from industry, the International Agricultural Research Centres, and universities and public research institutes from North and South, concluded that:

- Southern researchers and Northern private biotechnology companies should collaborate more, but only under some kind of umbrella of patent protection. Some internships for developing country researchers in US companies had already begun.

- Thailand and India were forging links between public and private sector researchers in their own countries.

- Greater efforts are needed to commercialise new biotechnologies emerging from developing country public laboratories.

- Private companies supported calls for clear regulation of biotechnology research and application, and denied they would use developing countries as under-regulated environments in which to pursue testing.

- Companies will not get involved in projects unless they are likely to make a profit.

- Smaller biotechnology companies are losing interest in vaccine development. So aid will be required to support it.

- IARCs should negotiate with the private sector for proprietary technologies, and establish pilot collaborations. Several are under way — notably between the potato research centre CIP in Peru and fast food companies interested in growing potatoes in developing countries for developing country chip markets.

- The need for companies to recover research and development costs through patented (or otherwise protected lines) "was recognised and understood".

- There was consensus that "unmodified, naturally occurring genes" should not be patented.

In a further report commissioned by USAID [2], Peter C. Hall and William H. Klausmeier, of the US Resource Development Foundation, looked at 193 submitted proposals for commercialising life sciences in Indonesia, the Philippines, Thailand, Kenya and Zimbabwe. They judged as likely to be profitable within 5-10 years only projects in Asia, dominated by several in Thailand — a country whose life-science research and development they assessed as "unsurpassed among developing countries in South-East Asia", and which was already actively engaged in commercialising this research.

Kenya is said to possess good national and international research facilities, directed by "highly competent" individuals, with several interesting potential technologies — such as micro-propagation of ornamental crops, animal vaccines and diagnostics, and aquaculture of the fish, tilapia. But the laboratories are severely limited by lack of funds, equipment, reagents and technical support staff, and Kenyan companies lack resources for research and development and concentrate on local markets, so commercial applications seem unlikely.

Zimbabwean researchers are developing a biotechnology research centre at the University of Zimbabwe, and, as in Kenya, much good research is under way. For example, the endod plant is being researched as a cheap molluscicide to control the snails that transmit schistosomiasis (commonly known as bilharzia). Research on ticks, on a vaccine against heartwater in livestock, and on micropropagation of coffee, potato and strawberry, is also under way.

The private sector is "very strong by most African standards," and has supported much biotechnology research. But, claim the authors of the USAID report, it is "severely limited" by African problems of poor communications with other African markets, foreign exchange controls, and limited air cargo space.

The Asian examples selected face fewer such limitations. The authors encourage Indonesia to pursue the commercial development of improved planting materials, the Philippines to pursue biogas production and the development of rhizobia (natural bacterial fertilisers).

Thailand, the biotechnical star of South-East Asia according to Hall and Klausmeier, could commercialise agar production from cultured seaweed, the bio-control of mosquito vectors, the production of brine and marine shrimps, and the culture of the alga Spirulina.

FOCUS: ON THE WORLD BANK SUPPORTING PRIVATE BIOTECHNOLOGY

The World Bank's advisors support private biotechnology as one of the main ways ahead. The Bank, with its large funds, is a potentially crucial actor in this field and already spends an estimated US$93 million a year on biotechnology. It appears to be advancing fast in efforts to establish a set of clear policy guidelines — at least in agriculture — for its own future support of biotechnology projects.

In a comprehensive study completed in May 1989 in association with Australian agencies and the International Service for National Agricultural Research (ISNAR) in The Hague, Bank advisors identified key issues in agricultural biotechnology and made extensive recommendations [3].

The advisors revealed a strong inclination towards support for the involvement of private industry — both indigenous and transnational — and for the use of patents.

Some key points:

- On the role of the private sector:
  — The new challenge to donor agencies, the IARCs and governments will be to develop innovative mechanisms to transfer technology from the industrial world's private sector to developing countries.
  — To help in this, new funding mechanisms should be created to encourage a greater role for the private sector, including multinationals and local private interests, in biotechnology in developing countries.

- On patents and the negotiation of technology transfers:
  — The lack of patent protection in many developing countries "is a major disincentive for private sector investments in biotechnology, both by local private sector companies and by transnational corporations".
  — The IARCs should be assisted in identifying advantages to be gained by patenting of their significant inventions, as a crucial card to play in negotiations with private sector interests.
  — The World Bank should develop negotiating skills in this area, and establish a "Biotechnology Transfer Unit" which would work on behalf of consortiums of developing countries, acting as a broker and advisor to obtain access to critical technologies likely to affect important commodities.

- On regulations covering the release of engineered organisms:
  — National and international regulations should be developed, and differences among them reduced. Legitimate public concern over environmental and health dangers could profoundly affect the development of biotechnology in different countries, and appropriate regulations are essential.
  — A "stringent, safe and efficient regulatory process" for new experiments and products will be an advantage for countries moving into biotechnology research or application.

- On the IARCs:
  — Several of the IARCs have taken little interest in biotechnology so far. But they must establish substantial programmes by the end of the century if they are to continue

to be useful and competitive.

— Donors should provide targeted biotechnology funds to the IARCs, to help them establish such programmes.

- On socio-economic issues:

— Biotechnology will increasingly affect marginal lands and their peoples which are under pressure to increase production, as yields of Green Revolution crops plateau.

— Donors should support research on the likely economic impact of biotechnology on developing countries.

- On agricultural constraints:

— Plant breeding capacity in many developing countries is very poor at present. Greatly enhanced indigenous plant breeding capacity will be essential for the adaptation and adoption of the new biotechnologies.

— International support to expand plant breeding capacity is therefore needed, together with research on local pests and diseases.

— Donors should sponsor wide-ranging analyses of commodities important to developing countries, to determine potential positive and negative impacts of biotechnology.

— In these studies, the expertise of scientists should be combined with that of economists who understand a given commodity, its market needs, and the likely impacts of any technical changes.

- On "orphan commodities":

— The World Bank should establish an "Orphan Commodities Programme" to support the application of biotechnology on crops and animals in which there is no substantial commercial interest in the industrial world.

It is already clear that the Bank will act on many of these points. David Hopper, Bank vice-president with responsibility for biotechnology, said in a free-ranging, informal address to the advisors' meeting in Canberra, Australia, in May 1989, that Bank involvement "is inevitable". He said the issue was clear — to feed the growing world population.

Relationships between advanced laboratories and clients will be "sensitive", said Hopper. Particularly in marginal lands, needs are very specific and local, and those who support and perform biotechnology research will have to take those needs into account: "We're going to have to work at how those relationships can be forged," he said.

FOCUS: ON KEEPING CHINESE HYBRID RICE EXCLUSIVE

A form of hybrid rice, capable of boosting harvests by up to 25%, now covers more than a third of China's 33 million hectares (81 million acres) of rice paddy. But the rice variety that allows its production — a so-called "male-sterile" line of rice that will not self-seed, and so may be easily crossed with another variety — is not being made available to the rest of Asia, where it could make a major contribution to increasing rice production.

The reason is that China has granted exclusive rights to seed production using the male-sterile lines to two US seed companies — which are in turn unwilling to release the know-how even though it has not proved profitable in Northern markets.

This was disclosed by B.D. Singh, the UN Food and Agriculture Organization's representative for Asia, at the FAO "Biotechnology and Third World Agriculture" meeting in Luxembourg in July 1989.

Singh had few details to offer, but Chinese scientists at the meeting described the situation as "more complicated". Panos has since investigated the issue...

Two multinational companies — Cargill Seeds and Ring Around Products Inc (a subsidiary of Occidental Petroleum) — are known to have licence agreements with the Chinese for seed development, production and marketing in specified countries.

It has not been possible to confirm the terms of either agreement with the Chinese Government, but the International Rice Research Institute (IRRI) in the Philippines believes Cargill holds rights for five countries. There are indications that the countries involved are Australia, Argentina, Thailand, Taiwan and the Philippines.

It is not known if the Occidental agreement with the Chinese follows a similar pattern to that with Cargill. But there are indications that, in addition to the US, Occidental's licence covers another nine countries: Japan, Italy, Egypt, Spain, Mexico, Portugal, North Korea, Indonesia and Brazil.

IRRI researchers were first alerted to the problem towards the end of 1987, when the Chinese Government unilaterally withdrew its support for an IRRI hybrid rice training course. Chinese involvement was planned under a 1979 agreement between IRRI and the Chinese Academy of Agricultural Sciences (CAAS).

But one week before the course, IRRI was informed of a 1981 agreement between the Chinese Government and two US companies — which forbade the sharing of information and materials concerning hybrid rice with other governments or with IRRI.

After the Chinese rebuff, IRRI has continued on its own with its

Harvesting and threshing rice in Yangshuo, Gangxi, China. */Sean Sprague/Panos Pictures*

hybrid rice development programme, and continues to supply China with information and materials as they become available. But the restrictions imposed by the Chinese mean that IRRI has been forced, without Chinese support, to breed its own rice hybrids adapted to tropical conditions.

Researchers at IRRI point out that this is a time-consuming process, and while making steady progress, the unavailability of Chinese know-how "has definitely slowed down the development of hybrid rice technology for the tropics".

According to Rice Tec — a US seed company which at one time worked for Ring Around, investigating the development of hybrid rice for the US market — Occidental originally thought that these varieties would have immediate commercial value on the US rice market. But the companies hit problems. It was not easy to make the hybrid seed, and even in China it was recognised as highly labour intensive. The harvested rice grains were also chalky and floury by American standards, and broke easily during milling.

Whereas cheap manual labour was available in China, there were serious problems in the US, with mechanisation of production to hold down labour costs. The new rice plants made few seeds, and without people to fertilise them manually, profits threatened to be lean.

According to rice specialist Gary Toenniessen of the Rockefeller Foundation: "In the late 1970s an early assessment carried out by an IRRI economist concluded that Chinese hybrid rices were fine for

China but wouldn't hold up in any free market economy."

Panos sought, and received, information about the programme from senior sources at Ring Around. But lawyers of the parent, Occidental Petroleum, then wrote to Panos saying that the company did not wish to make any statement.

Other sources, however, confirmed that Ring Around Products have continued in their efforts to develop hybrid rice suitable for the US market — and have patented a hybrid rice seed production process. On 16 August 1988, Ring Around took out US Patent Number 4,764,643 for a "route to hybrid rice production".

A USAID official was concerned that patents on the technology were blocking its future commercial use — because the patent holders had not found the technology profitable or effective in Northern markets. The official told Panos that, if this were true, "the company should be encouraged to release its technology into the public domain".

The Chinese Government indicated to irate FAO officials in early-1989 that it hoped to help release the technology.

But even if China does have the legal power to do so (having contracted the technology to the companies), some commentators have been sceptical of Chinese intentions. The strategic value of being first in the race to develop and patent commercial rice hybrids is high. And China, they say, has a reputation for being astute about retaining control of germplasm — valuable plants — and has always been reluctant to make them available internationally.

Neil Rutger, of the US Department of Agriculture, says: "Research scientists have known for 25 years that, if you could develop a high-yielding, disease-resistant hybrid, this would open the way for proprietary control," thus confirming Pioneer Hi-Bred's views expressed earlier in this chapter.

Henk Hobbelink, of Seeds Action Network, an international non-governmental pressure group, adds: "Once hybrids have been developed that are commercially viable in the rice bowls of Asia, the interest of private companies will increase dramatically. Public funding for seed production programmes will be replaced by private capital. With this, the public control of a major food crop would cease.

"You can look to India to see how fast this occurs," he says. "In 1988, India started a new seed policy. Previously all seed production was done publicly. [Now farmers are allowed to import seeds from abroad.] Within a year at least three agro-industrial multinationals — Pepsi Cola, Royal Sluis, Pioneer — have moved in to take up the market. There is no indication that this will in the long run benefit the bulk of Indian farmers. Indeed the lessons of the Green Revolution suggest quite the opposite."

And, adds Rutger: "So-called 'two-line hybrids' are already in existence in China. The Chinese claim they will have them in use commercially by 1991. They have also told IRRI they will not be releasing these, either. One can't help wondering if a US company will turn out to have exclusive rights to the germplasm and development of these."

China, like many other developing countries, clearly wishes to make a profit on the marketing of its own technological developments by selling the rights to private companies.

But, as Rockefeller's Gary Toenniessen says: "The down side of the privatisation of biotechnology research is that the international research system based upon collaborative efforts will inevitably suffer.

"Every country wants to get in on a piece of the action. But if you allow a multinational company to take out a patent on the development of your germplasm then there will inevitably be restriction placed upon it [the country] to protect the investment a company makes."

Many IARCs are increasingly turning to private companies for research funding. Toenniessen believes that the Chinese hybrid rice experience will have a profound effect on IARCs in future: "It is bound to inform their willingness to get involved with private industry."

FOCUS ON INDIA'S 'PRO-POOR' BIOTECHNOLOGY

Among developing countries, India is better placed than most to capitalise on biotechnology. It has large numbers of scientists, is fast acquiring expertise in DNA technology, and has a well-developed indigenous industry. So how is it mixing public and private interests?

As biotechnology's potential for improving health and raising food production became clear, the Indian Government decided to give biotechnology the same high priority it gave atomic energy in the 1950s. A Department of Biotechnology was created in 1986 and was brought under the Ministry of Science, which is in the charge of the Prime Minister. The 1989-90 budget for the department stood at US$35 million.

To date, India has invested about US$120 million in the biotechnology programme. It will rise to US$650 million during the eighth plan (1990-95). According to the department, indigenous biotechnology research is expected to lead to the generation of products worth US$1,500 million per year, beginning in 1995.

The Department of Biotechnology sees biotechnology as essentially "pro-poor". Unlike the Green Revolution, which relied on costly inputs and hence excluded poor farmers, biotechnology promises to decrease input costs and is hence not anti-poor, it says. India's view is that biotechnology will be to poor farmers what the Green Revolution was to the rich.

Currently, three-quarters of the Department of Biotechnology's budget is spent on research and development which the department claims will result in products relevant to the poor in India.

But India's emerging biotechnology faces much competition from imports from abroad, and is also hampered by Indian industry's unwillingness to trust Indian biotechnology.

Competition from imports

Industry in general is cautious about commercialising Indian-developed biotechnology products because of the notion that they are inferior to imported ones. Instead, they are falling over themselves to enter into collaboration with overseas biotechnology firms.

The Department of Biotechnology has been vested with the power to accept or reject proposals from foreign biotechnology companies for marketing their products, or proposals from Indian firms for collaboration with foreign firms. In one year alone the department received 80 applications for foreign collaboration.

"I cannot stop foreign companies entering the Indian market if they have really good products to offer," says the department chief. If there is a miracle crop or a new vaccine, he says, it would be unjustified to deny its benefit to Indians; whether or not India should import biotechnology products and know-how, would ultimately have to be a political decision.

The spectre of biotechnology invasion from abroad is very real given India's poor track record of converting laboratory processes into commercial products. For example, no industry came forward to commercialise the production of cheap, nitrogen-fixing blue-green algae starter cultures, which poor farmers can use as a substitute for expensive nitrogen fertiliser on their rice fields. This may result in much more expensive cultures, made locally by a US-based firm, taking over the market.

"Our prime task is to get industries involved," says Dr G.S. Venkataraman, Research Director of the Indian Agricultural Research Institute (IARI) in Hyderabad, "otherwise everything we do now will turn out to be purely academic. We will end up preparing a market for foreign companies to exploit, and the dependency will be harmful in the long run."

But the link between research laboratories and industry is missing. Except for a few firms, industry's response to the Department of Biotechnology's programme is virtually zero.

For example, promising technology packages for making immunodiagnostic kits for pregnancy, typhoid, filariasis and amoebiasis, have been developed by Indian laboratories. The typhoid kit (which the USSR wants to import) takes nine hours to reveal if a patient is positive and another six hours to name the antibiotic to which his strain is sensitive. Current methods take four days. "Our kits are cheaper than imported ones," says Dr G. P. Talwar, Director of the National Institute of Immunology (NII) in New Delhi, which developed all except the filariasis kit, which came from the Mahatma Gandhi Institute in Wardha.

But Indian industries are not taking risks. It was only after great persuasion that four drug companies agreed to manufacture the immunodiagnostic kits. And they agreed only on condition that the Department of Biotechnology would buy every kit made in the first two years of manufacture.

This type of attitude, and total neglect of research and development on "downstream processing", will impede conversion of laboratory processes into commercial products. India also lacks the biochemical engineering base which is essential to take a product from the research laboratory to the market.

According to India's Science Minister, K.R. Narayanan, biotechnology is a garden of Eden, "but there is no garden without a snake in it". He is particularly wary of misuse of biotechnology and India becoming a slave to multinationals. "We have to turn to biotechnology in a systematic way with a sense of urgency, and within a well-thought out policy framework for self-reliance," he recently told a conference. Funding will be no problem, but in return he urged Indian scientists to produce products on their own "without waiting for the fruits of research and development from advanced nations".

This is a tall order considering the fact that Indian industry is sluggish and that the department faces competition from abroad in virtually every product that it intends to develop locally.

The outlook is not entirely bleak, however. A biotechnological product which has found an industrial producer is a powerful mosquito-killing biopesticide — Biocide-S. It is a strain of the bacterium *Bacillus sphaericus*, developed by scientists of the biotechnology centre at Anna University in Madras. This strain contains a high concentration of a toxin deadly for mosquito larvae.

Formulations of Biocide-S that spread on the water surface have

Mary's DNA fingerprint

A DNA probe developed for DNA fingerprinting is the first Indian biotechnology product to go commercial.

Parents of five-year-old Mary were taken to court in 1988 by a couple who claimed that she was their kidnapped child. A court in Madras finally restored the child to her real parents on the evidence provided by DNA fingerprints.

This was the first time the technique of DNA fingerprinting had been used in an Indian court.

Just like a real fingerprint, DNA fingerprints can identify an individual unambiguously. And they can also do more. Because they are based on certain patterns of DNA sequences, and since a person's DNA is inherited from his or her parents, and is also to some extent shared with that of his or her brothers, sisters and other blood relatives, they can also establish family relationships.

DNA fingerprinting is based on the discovery that there are parts of human chromosomes where short sequences, around 15 bases long, are repeated again and again. The number of blocks of repeats and the number of repeats in each block vary from person to person and are virtually unique to an individual.

A small sample of DNA extracted from a drop of blood, semen or other tissue, can be treated in such a way that the number of blocks and repeats is revealed as a pattern of bands. Radioactive DNA probes which match the repeat sequence are used to reveal the pattern, which looks very like a supermarket bar code. Except in the case of identical twins, the probability of two "bar codes" being alike is very slight.

The DNA probe that solved Mary's case was developed by Lalji Singh at the Centre for Cellular and Molecular Biology (CCMB) in Hyderabad.

With the Madras court having set a precedent, dozens of cases of paternity dispute and 15 cases of burglary, rape and murder have been referred to the Centre. Its director, Dr Pushpa Bhargava, predicts that by 2010, having a DNA fingerprint will become a statutory requirement like a birth certificate.

The government is now considering setting up an autonomous US$6 million facility, to be named the National Centre for DNA Fingerprinting and Diagnostics, for commercially exploiting the technology. This will provide a fingerprinting service free of charge to the police and for a fee of US$80 to other government agencies and the public. Foreigners will pay US$160 — low enough, it is hoped, to attract a large number of customers from abroad.

The problem facing such a service, however, will be to prove its quality and objectivity. Contamination of samples with, for example, the experimenters' own DNA, can confuse results: in a recent US court case, genetic fingerprinting evidence was overruled as unsound as the scientists had not been strict enough with their experimental methods.

been successfully field-tested by the Malaria Research Centre in Delhi. Field trials by the Madras municipal corporation last year showed 100% larval deaths in 24 hours, with a dose as low as 1.25 mg/cc. The effect lasted for as long as 30 days. A production facility will now be set up by Southern Petrochemicals Industrial Corporation.

A case where private industry has led the way is in the tissue culture of cardamom — a valuable spice. The tissue culture technology has been perfected by two private companies (A.V. Thomes and Co in Cochin and Hindustan Lever in Bombay). By July 1990, tissue-cultured cardamom will be planted in 100 one-hectare farmers' plots in the states of Kerala, Karnataka and Tamil Nadu. Currently, cardamom productivity is 50 kg/hectare or one-fifth of that of Guatemala, India's competitor in the international cardamom market. The tissue-cultured plants should yield six times more and could potentially make India the number one producer of cardamom.

But cardamom is a crop grown by rich farmers, which is possibly why it has attracted private industry. Poor farmers with marginal land holdings are expected to benefit more from the application of tissue culture to bamboo used for house construction throughout north-east India. This, like almost all work that benefits the poor, is publicly funded. Normally, bamboo seeds are available during flowering cycles that vary from 20 to 60 years. Under a project funded by the Department of Biotechnology, scientists at Delhi University have perfected the technique for mass production of three species of bamboo, completely eliminating the need for seed sets. Over 12,000 plantlets produced by tissue culture have been made ready for planting. According to the department, more than 250 plantlets could be accommodated in one hectare and the annual return could be US$1,550, "which is substantial for poor farmers".

The impact of biotechnology on India's poor farmers will ultimately depend on who penetrates the market — Indian companies using farmer-friendly appropriate technologies developed in India, or foreign companies with an eye on profits and less concerned about whether their products benefit the rich or the poor. It is the political system and not the scientists which has the final say.

The seed import policy

Experience of one recent government decision leads Indian agricultural scientists, at least, not to be too optimistic. Great controversy was created in agricultural circles by the Indian Government's recent lifting of a long-time ban on the unrestricted import of seeds from abroad. Previously, only selective import of seeds for use in breeding programmes was allowed. Now, farmers and seed merchants are free to import seed for planting.

The seed import policy was introduced in haste without a debate by agricultural scientists, and has shattered the morale of India's plant breeders who have given the country the highest yielding sugar-cane, potato and grapes, and the world's first hybrid cotton.

Even the government's own Department of Biotechnology was not consulted over the seeds policy, but was presented with a political fait accompli.

The rule that came into effect from 1 October 1988 permits the import of seeds of a wide range of crops and ornamentals under what is known as open general licence. Within a few weeks of the policy being announced, some 150 companies obtained permission and at least 32 of them have imported seeds.

Government scientists, who do not want to be quoted, say the seeds policy will reverse the gains of the Green Revolution and make Indian agriculture parasitic. Their attitude is summed up by Dr Amir Singh, founder President of the Indian Society of Seed Technology. "In the course of time the entire agriculture will become dependent on supplies of seeds from abroad ... Our farmers will buy them at higher prices under the impression they are better than indigenously bred varieties," he has said.

The gains expected from India's biotechnology programme may be offset by the seeds policy. The biotechnology programme is aimed at reducing input costs, but the imported seeds will be expensive. According to Dr P.K. Agrawal, head of the Seed Technology Division at IARI, "75% of Indian farmers will have no money to buy the seeds".

"The seeds policy will only widen the disparity between the rich and the poor," says Mr P.K. Tandon, Joint Secretary of the All-India Farmers' Union.

With the lifting of import restrictions, multinationals will find it easier to import genetically engineered seeds, when they are ready. And, now that multinationals are assured of seed business, their lobby in India is asking the government to introduce plant breeders' rights.

This is opposed by many agricultural scientists, 900 of whom recently submitted a petition to the Speaker of the Indian Parliament calling for the withdrawal of the seeds policy and rejection of any move to introduce plant breeders' rights.

International collaboration

What seems at first sight to be beneficial international collaboration can also be controversial, raising fears of exploitation. A biotechnology programme that has remained on hold for more than two years is the controversial Vaccine Action Programme (VAP), a joint Indian-US agreement, signed in July 1987.

According to the Department of Biotechnology, which signed the agreement, VAP had two aims: training Indian scientists in the field of vaccinology, and combating diseases like cholera, polio, typhoid, diarrhoea, rabies and hepatitis through new and more effective vaccines.

Controversy arose out of the fear that Indians would be used as guinea-pigs by US firms for trying out products which are difficult to test in the West due to rigid controls. Among other things, the agreement proposed the testing of genetically engineered vaccines on Indians and the collection of clinical material and epidemiological data by US researchers, ostensibly for adapting the vaccines to Indian conditions.

The second point raised concern over access of American laboratories — some of them involved with US defence projects on biological warfare — to the militarily sensitive data pertaining to disease and immunity patterns of Indians.

Critics also argued that high-tech vaccines were not the answer to disease caused primarily by poor sanitation and hygiene.

Although some of these issues have been resolved, VAP is yet to take off, one reason being the unresolved question of protection of intellectual property rights. The US would like to patent the products emerging out of VAP, but India — which allows patents only on processes but not on products — has steadfastly refused to change its patent law or to sign the Paris Convention.

CHAPTER 11

GENETIC RESOURCES

Developing countries can claim to be rich in one thing at least: genetic resources.

Robert May, a leading biomathematician, has demonstrated that tropical forests must contain around 30 million species of insect (of which only a million or so are even described by science, let alone investigated) [1]. Previous guesses had put the figure at only 3 million.

The number of tropical forest micro-organisms — bacteria, viruses, and fungi — will be even greater than 30 million, because the number of environmental nooks and crannies — "niches" — that create species' differences rises as the scale gets smaller. These organisms provide a vast untapped source of potential biocontrol agents against insects, plant diseases and weeds.

Even on the larger scale, many species of tropical trees and plants remain to be described and investigated, say botanists. And as for the ecological relationships of all these species and their genes — for example, the associations with insects and fungi that determine the productivity of a wild Brazil nut tree — essentially nothing is known.

It is not only tropical forests that are rich in species and their genes. Famine-ridden Ethiopia is actually a "Vavilov centre of diversity" for cereal genes — one of several, mostly developing country, world centres of origin of useful crop genes, first described by Soviet botanist N. I. Vavilov.

Only a small proportion of these genes, in tropical forests or the Vavilov centres, can be said to have been securely collected and stored. Most are still in the forest and the field: they are under increasing threat from the disappearance of virgin forest habitat and from the displacement of indigenous local crop varieties, in which there is much genetic variation, by improved varieties with a much more uniform genetic base.

Indigenous genetic resources are potentially worth billions. Green Revolution genes added US$2 billion of value annually to wheat grown in Asia, and US$1.5 billion to rice. A wild Turkish wheat plant supplied genes giving disease resistance to a commercial variety now worth US$50 million a year in the US alone. Nearly one-quarter of the genes used in US wheat come from Mexico — but Mexico profits nothing. The US National Cancer Institute has long been running a US$8 million annual natural product cancer drug screening programme, looking among other things at tropical chemicals [2].

One-quarter of the world's pharmaceutical products are derived from tropical forests, and the search is on for more. Among many such ventures, India and Germany are collaborating to tissue-culture rare Indian medicinal plants. And the UK company Biotics Ltd is helping countries investigate their tropical plants for new pharmaceuticals, by acting as a broker for the countries with Northern chemicals companies [3].

These companies, at their own cost, will investigate the activity of the plants. Biotics is drawing up contracts under which, if marketable products emerge, the companies will pay the source country a lump sum or "appropriate" royalties on production in exchange for world exclusive rights on the products.

Biotics has been planning such deals in countries like Nigeria, Ghana, Kenya, the Seychelles and Thailand. Leading Western pharmaceutical companies like Beechams, Rhône Poulenc, Glaxo, Hoechst, NOVO and Sandoz, are said to have shown interest in such arrangements. However, there is concern over whether, in the end, the Third World countries involved will benefit fairly. And the Biotics exercise is only one among several other such ventures, many with less concern for equity.

What does biotechnology have to do with this? Biotechnology is:

- Widening and deepening the commercial and public interest in the collection of genes to be used in genetic engineering.

- Offering alternative methods of production of new tropical products (for example, the industrial tissue culture of some root that produces a useful drug, or the cloning of rattan vines to increase numbers of vines in a forest area).

- Developing genetically uniform cloned "super-species" which will displace farmers' genetically variable crops and animals in marginal lands, reducing available genetic diversity in the Vavilov centres.

But above all, it is:

- Strengthening the resolve of developing countries to protect their interests in these resources.

- Providing new techniques for collecting and conserving germplasm.

THE FIGHT FOR FARMERS' RIGHTS

"The South must aggressively safeguard its most important bargaining tool — the plant and animal germplasm that comprise the raw materials for biotechnology," says Pat Roy Mooney, a genetic resources activist.

Some countries have arrived at Mooney's conclusions for themselves — among them Ethiopia, one of the classic Vavilov centres of crop diversity. In a well-resourced national gene bank, built with West German aid, farmers' varieties of important crops (such as teff and coffee, which originated in Ethiopia), are being exhaustively collected and stored. The International Board for Plant Genetic Resources (IBPGR) in Rome, Italy, describes the bank as "extremely well run... all concerned should be heartily congratulated". But Ethiopia embargoes exports of this national germplasm, particularly of economic crops such as coffee.

Ethiopia has thus challenged the open-door policy of free world access to genetic resources of the IBPGR, and of the West Germans, who expected to receive duplicates of the Ethiopian barley collection [5].

Thaumatin brings riches only to some

In recent years, Nigeria has seen increased activity by germplasm collectors from developed countries. But for many years before, local researchers were collecting the country's genetic resources. The largest collections are at the International Institute of Tropical Agriculture (IITA) in Ibadan, with smaller private collections scattered throughout universities and research institutes.

There are collections of raffia and other palms, yam, cassava, and hundreds of species of common herbs, trees, shrubs and grasses, as well as germplasm collections of the introduced crop plants — such as maize and cacao — which are grown in the region.

Collections include the wild bambarra nut (*Vigna subterranea*) from the arid northern savannahs, made after the nut had been virtually wiped off the land elsewhere 15 years ago by the widespread cultivation of the common groundnut *Arachis hypogea*. There are many thousands of accessions of germplasm from some of the many species of palm trees native to Nigeria. Some 40 years ago, Malaysian agronomists took away from Nigeria seedlings from just one species of palm, to use in becoming the world's leading palm oil producer.

But without industrial infrastructure and sufficient funding to research and exploit indigenous genetic resources, the benefits often go abroad. When, some 10 years ago, researchers at the University of Ife identified the sweetener thaumatin in the berries of *Thaumatococcus danielli*, which is common in the forests of that part of Nigeria, no industry was interested even in using the fruit as a sweetener.

But today, the gene for thaumatin, which is a protein weight-for-weight some 1,600 times sweeter than sugar, has been cloned, and is being used for the industrial production of sweetener in the confectionery industry. Patents on the process have been registered, but the people from whose lands the gene was obtained are still as poor as ever.

Moreover, there are many examples of what might be called gene
plunder — for example, of the cowpea trypsin inhibitor gene. Here, a
natural African insect-killing gene was discovered and extracted in
Britain, where the gene is being commercialised. The cloned gene was
returned, free, to its source in Nigeria. But it does not appear that any
profits from the gene will be returned to Africa, any more than they
will from the gene for the sweetener, thaumatin.

In Zimbabwe, research is going on to develop an animal vaccine
against ticks. Australian scientists are on similar tracks, but Zimbabwe
is unlikely to release its tick genes to the Australians for fear they will
move faster — and end up selling their own genes back to them in the
form of a vaccine.

Meanwhile, pressure is building for international support for
developing countries to get more deeply involved in such
negotiations, perhaps through a World Bank "international
biotechnology acquisitions unit", whose establishment is now under
consideration. Developing countries that are suspicious of such
initiatives will have to take up the challenge to establish their own
more independent forums.

Alternatively, negotiation for returns on genes could also be done
by donors on behalf of developing countries: the purchase, for such
purposes, of a genetic technology, could be just as good or better than

buying infrastructure or a dam.

To deal with such conflicts, and at the same time to make world genetic resources available to all who want or need it while giving an equitable return to source countries, the UN Food and Agriculture Organization (FAO) has established the Intergovernmental Commission on Plant Genetic Resources which is attempting to iron out the rights and wrongs of the case.

The Commission's basic position is that there is value in a technology; and that there is value in the germplasm that the technology uses. The first is owned by the technology maker; the second, by developing countries whose farmers, over centuries, may have selected the genes in question (unless the genes are wild ones). Such supposed ownership of genes has been known as "farmers' rights" over the genes. It is now expressed in the "International Undertaking" which recognises the rights of technology and donors of germplasm to be compensated for their contributions.

One fundamental problem, says the Commission secretary, Dr J. Esquinas-Alcazar, is that "in 99% of cases you will not identify who should benefit" as the source of the germplasm, because the genes will have come from sources that cross national boundaries. "The answer," he says, "is that these genes belong to humanity. So biotechnologists who use the genes should pay fees into an international fund."

This fund would benefit developing countries by paying for the protection of plant genetic resources, and for the research and creation of improved seeds for developing country conditions.

Private biotechnology and seed companies that need the genes for their breeding programmes would also benefit, because the scheme would help preserve, and open legitimate access to, developing country germplasm.

A US government source, however, believes the FAO position to be "too polarised", as returns to the fund are being sought from existing proprietary lines (such as US wheat with its 23% Mexican content). "No one's going to agree to that," the source said. Meanwhile, the US has not joined the intergovernmental commission, but is staying on the sidelines as an observer; until the US joins, the Commission will have no teeth, as the US represents the world's largest group of breeders.

In the November 1989 annual meeting of the governmental body of the FAO, however, there was some progress on the issue. For the first time, delegates agreed to a wording of the definition of farmers' rights, and of the International Undertaking. Both were still loose, but admitted the basic principles for which countries have been pressing.

According to Jack Kloppenburg of the Department of Rural

Sociology, College of Agricultural and Life Sciences, Madison, USA — who is a pro-Third World activist on these issues — the agreement had been "really surprising". The main points accepted by developing countries and industrialised countries alike were:

- The existence of plant breeders' rights — that allow property protection by Northern breeders — were "not incompatible" with the Undertaking. (This was a concession by the South.)

- The "enormous contribution of farmers" to breeding useful varieties would be recognised in the concept of farmers' rights. (This was a concession by the North.)

- "To reflect the responsibilities of those countries which have benefited most from the use of germplasm [that is, the North], the international fund would benefit from further contributions by adhering governments." Such wording is vague, but, says Kloppenburg, "it opens doors".

- "The benefits to be derived under the International Undertaking should be limited to the adherents of the undertaking."

The significance of the last point is that if international gene banks were to come under the auspices of the FAO, as some delegations are recommending, then only adherents of the Undertaking, and thus contributors to the international fund, would benefit from the gene banks. This clause could therefore become the "teeth" of the whole Undertaking.

Meanwhile, however, the US and other major plant breeding countries actually remain outsiders — observers, and not members of the Intergovermental Commission, and so non-adherents to the Undertaking. They may join, however, at some future date. According to Kloppenburg, in the US the American Seed Trade Association is "calling the shots". He describes some of its principal members as "out of the mid-West and knowing nowhere else... calling all talk of development 'communism'".

It may take some years, therefore, before farmers' rights are implemented, Kloppenburg believes. In a related initiative, but one which to some extent competes with that of the FAO, the United Nations Environment Programme (UNEP) together with the US-based World Resources Institute and the Swiss-based International Union for the Conservation of Nature and Natural Resources, are drafting a "Biodiversity Convention" which aims to protect genetic resources world-wide; but its emphasis appears to be on the natural world itself, and the creation of parks and exclusion zones, rather than on the needs of the Third World poor.

New techniques for genetic conservation

Biotechnology is being used to help conserve genetic resources in several ways: in new methods for the collection and storage of genes (now not just as seeds, but also as tissue cultures); the elimination of diseases in the stock; long-term storage; and distribution to users. So explains Lesley Withers, responsible for biotechnology at the International Board for Plant Genetic Resources (IBPGR).

Collection: It is not always straightforward to collect genes by collecting seed. Coconut seed, for example, is the coconut — which is difficult to collect and store in any numbers. The same problem affects avocado. Many plants, such as grasses important for cattle (forage grasses), produce seed only with difficulty (they are said to be

Harvesting coconuts in
Tamil Nadu, India.
The dried coconut
pulp, know as copra, is
a valuable export
product. Coconut
production could be
quadrupled by cloning
the most productive
trees. /Ron
Giling/Panos Pictures

"shy seeders"), or rarely, necessitating expensive searches for seed in remote areas (such as the Amazon Basin for cacao).

The solution for such plants has been the development of a form of "in-field tissue culture". The collector takes a viable portion of the plant (in the coconut, one of the three eyes or a leaf bud), sterilises it in an antiseptic solution, and pops it into a sterile bottle of salt water. It can stay there for up to a couple of weeks, until the collector returns to the laboratory, when the tissue can be placed on special media for culture.

The details of the technique must be worked out for each plant, but it is now working (and will make a major impact in germplasm collection) in coconut (although as yet the tissue culture will not divide and propagate), and experiments are in progress on avocado, cacao, prunus (plum etc) and grape.

Diseases: Tissue culture can be used to clean-up germplasm, and eliminate pests and diseases which do not survive tissue culture conditions. Monoclonal antibodies and DNA probes can be used for precise "indexing" — diagnosing the exact diseases present in a given tissue culture, seed, plant, or tree, even if symptoms are not visible.

Storage: Germplasm is traditionally stored as seed, or as plants in plantations, or a combination of both. Some seeds do not store well, are sterile or have very poor germination rates. Some plants are difficult to grow in plots. Then tissue culture can come into its own — storing the plant cells as tissue on a growth medium in a flask or test-tube.

The method risks variation arising in the tissue culture, but it is possible to slow variation by limiting growth with low temperature and hormone treatment. And, in theory, variation can also be detected, and cultures that have suffered it can be eliminated.

Tissue culture would be useful for storing sweet potato, banana and plantain (which are sterile), apples (the cultivated varieties are clones), cocoa, coconut, avocado, mango and many other tropical fruits. However, coconut tissue has proved difficult — it will not divide and multiply as well as its relative, oil palm.

The technique is proving easiest for roots, tubers and tropical fruits, and worst for woody plants and trees. However, even where the technique does work, "we don't know how long such cultures will last," says Withers. The longest-lived — 10 years in culture so far — is potato.

Deep-freezing at liquid nitrogen temperatures of minus 196 °C (cryopreservation) is another possible storage technique, but much less well developed. There are projects to apply it to coconut, cassava, banana and plantain, and studies of genetic stability under cryopreservation in potato shoot tips and maize (embryos and shoots) are in progress.

Distribution of germplasm is limited by the danger of transmitting plant diseases, and worm and insect pests to new environments, and so by the amounts of disease-free seed or plants that can be created, tested and transported. Biotechnology is providing more certified disease-free tissue and plants and — through tissue culture — reducing the physical volumes of materials that need to be moved.

Tissue culture distribution is now routine for potato, cassava and yam.

CHAPTER 12

ENVIRONMENTAL ISSUES

PUTTING ENVIRONMENTAL RISKS IN CONTEXT

Current biotechnology is a combination of power and ignorance: power over the genes, but relative ignorance of biological interactions between genes at the level of the cell, between cells at the level of the organism, and between organisms in the surrounding ecosystem.

So, given its power and its ignorance, is biotechnology dangerous?

In one sense, genetic engineering is only an amplification of what farmers have long done — to shuffle genes through breeding to create useful plants and animals, or to move a useful plant or animal from one continent to another.

But some groups, such as the Foundation for Economic Trends led by US environmentalist Jeremy Rifkin, oppose most, if not all, aspects of biotechnology. They do so partly on the moral ground that it represents an unwarranted and unnatural tampering with the genetic make-up of living things, tending to reduce animal and plant life to the status of commodities for human consumption. They contend that there are many ways in which biological systems can benefit us without having to tamper with their genetic code, and that we need to develop ways of working with nature rather than controlling it if we are to avoid threatening the viability of the planet.

Other scientists, especially ecologists, as well as environmentalists, while not condemning biotechnology and genetic engineering out of hand, urge extreme caution, especially over the release of novel organisms into the environment [1].

The practical issues

There are two main practical issues: the containment, in laboratories and industry, of modified organisms; and the deliberate release of genetically engineered organisms.

Containment regulations began soon after 1975, when a conference of concerned scientists was held in Asilomar, California to sound the

Salvinia – the water weed that clones itself, and once clogged the Kariba Dam in Africa. *Nigel Cattlin/Holt Studios*

alert about the potential dangers of genetic engineering. This led to stringent guidelines, of which the best-known are those prepared by the US National Institutes of Health (NIH), demanding several different levels of physical and biological containment of modified organisms. The original scientific concern about simple gene operations has since decreased, but most institutions — North and South — have regulations based on the increasingly relaxed NIH guidelines.

If containment is an old issue, deliberate environmental release of genetically engineered organisms is the new and potentially more serious one. The "old-fashioned" accidental or deliberate introduction of animals and plants from one continent to another has created ecological nightmares in the past: the spread of rabbits — and more recently cane toads — in Australia, for example, and the virtual extinction of some indigenous species by competition and predation by introduced animals. In Africa, Kariba weed — a South American water plant that grows rapidly by division (cloning itself) — choked the Kariba Dam on the Zambesi River and several other water bodies until a predator beetle was discovered that would devour it.

Most countries now have strict quarantine regulations governing the movement of plants and animals to prevent the introduction of foreign pests and diseases, or of insects and microbes that may become troublesome if introduced into countries where their natural predators are absent.

Proponents of genetic engineering consider that, in most cases, the introduction of one or two genes into a plant, animal or microbe, is unlikely to produce anything as potentially dangerous as some of these previous introductions of "alien" organisms.

But ecologists are more cautious. A committee of the Ecological Society of America, for example, while broadly welcoming the benefits that biotechnology could bring, urges caution in environmental releases, pointing out that, "although the capability to produce precise genetic alterations increases confidence that unintended changes in the genome [the total genetic make-up of an organism] have not occurred, precise genetic characterisation does not ensure that all ecologically important aspects of the phenotype [the biological properties of an organism] can be predicted for the environments into which an organism will be introduced [2]."

Submitting evidence to the UK Royal Commission on Environmental Pollution, the UK Genetics Forum, a collection of scientists, academics, environmentalists, consumer representatives, and animal welfarists, has recommended that "a partial moratorium on the release of genetically engineered organisms to the environment should be instituted. It should run until ecological research has significantly improved our ability to assess the risks involved, and a full public debate has been stimulated. During this period genetically engineered organisms should only be released to the environment in order to further our understanding of their behaviour in natural systems [3]."

It is probably true to say that, among scientists at least, the worry is not so much *how* a particular genetically changed organism has been produced, but what it might do when released.

Comments the Ecological Society of America: "Genetically engineered organisms should be evaluated and regulated according to their biological properties (phenotypes), rather than according to the genetic techniques used to produce them."

There are, however, certain distinctions between "old-fashioned" gene movements and the products of genetic engineering, which could add to the risks:

- The short time-scale on which genes are being moved and introduced will allow little time for testing or ecological adjustment. There are fears that pressure from the increasing number of planned releases, and pressure from industry, will lead to regulatory bodies relaxing testing procedures for categories they deem innocuous. But in the present state of knowledge, ecologists argue, no genetically engineered organism (or indeed, any introduced "alien" organism) should be considered ecologically neutral.

- The great variety of genes being shuffled: genetic engineering is allowing the movement of genes among organisms as distantly related as plants and humans, thus producing real genetic novelties whose ecological effects could be hard to predict from past experience.

- The degree to which genes introduced into one species could eventually move into another species, by natural, if very rare, means of interspecies gene transfer, are so far quite unpredictable. The movement of genes between different micro-organisms is a particular concern here, as the species barriers between different sorts of bacteria, for example, are far less clear-cut than in animals and plants. Novel genes, such as those for herbicide resistance, might also move from some crop plants into a weedy relative during rare instances of interspecies crossing — a highly undesirable outcome.

- The ownership of the technologies is largely private and oriented to short-term profit, in industries only just becoming aware of the need for environmental protection.

The risks, however small, must be taken seriously because:

- In their nature, genetic systems — like Kariba weed — multiply themselves. The risk of a replicating, dangerous genetic system is thus of a potentially different order than, say, the release of a finite amount of oil from a tanker. It has to be assumed that, once released, living organisms cannot be recalled. Because of their genetic novelty it might be even harder to find ways of eradicating a "mistake".

- Human error will continue for ever, and engineering is often less a science than a process of learning from audacious mistakes. Since more and more gene transfers are going to be done, over wider and wider species barriers, in more and more varied ecologies, with little knowledge of local conditions, it seems certain that there will one day be some mistake — some release that will eventually be regretted, even if it is no more dangerous than Kariba weed.

- The general public perceives the technology to be risky. It has many of the hallmarks of nuclear radiation: its operations are invisible, and in the hands of experts whom the public may not trust.

Hubert Zandstra, research director of the International Rice Research Institute (IRRI) in the Philippines, says that "the public trust of scientists vanished with Chernobyl and Bhopal — I saw it fall away — there's a big gulf to bridge".

After a controversy over an IRRI experiment with rice blast fungus, the Philippines Government has banned the import of DNA probes etc until proper regulations are in force. "We can't import mapping probes from Cornell because of the restrictions," says Lesley Sitch, who runs the interspecies crossing programme at IRRI.

Scientists are therefore looking for a certain amount of media help. The public will inevitably get to know what is happening — "and if that knowledge comes by rumour, the reaction will be much worse," says Ellen Messer of the World Hunger Programme, who has been studying these issues at Brown University, USA. "The information must come from the scientists," she adds.

Meanwhile, releases are now becoming more common in several countries — particularly France, where the environmentalists' foothold is small, and where, traditionally, experts and engineers enjoy great respect and are given greater licence than elsewhere. According to a report by John Hodgson in the first edition of the magazine *Scientific European* [4], during the last three years over 50 separate releases have been made in France, with 20 in 1989 alone — considerably more than the whole of the rest of Europe, and more than in the United States, where regulation is stricter and public opposition vociferous.

In developing countries, there are added complications:

- The technology is often in the hands of an economically strong foreigner — usually a multinational company or a foreign government — whose motives may be suspected.

- The lax or non-existent regulations controlling biotechnology releases in Third World countries could be attractive to companies or institutions wishing to test products that cannot be tested in the tougher regulatory climate of their home country.

Many experts argue that the speed at which countries can establish effective regulations on the release of genetically engineered organisms will limit the speed at which biotechnology can be applied to developing country crops. Others say the recognition of patents will set the limits.

Ecological and physiological studies will have to be made of the risks of the genes "escaping" from engineered varieties, and entering wild plants (the risk of herbicide resistance is the most obvious); and national decisions will be needed about where it is safest to run trials, and what studies should be done before allowing a particular release.

Technical "biosafety committees", preferably with lay local representation, will also be needed in research laboratories to adjudge — and where appropriate, approve — the movement of the materials of the trade. The lack of such assessment processes (and consequent ad hoc regulation) "is beginning to be the major constraint on our work", says the research director of IRRI.

These reflections lead to four basic conclusions:

- **National and international regulations are needed**, and watch-dog bodies — with public representation to recognise public concern — are necessary to oversee research institutes and production facilities to minimise the number, and consequences, of biotechnical mistakes. Such regulations and bodies will also clear what will otherwise be a tangled path for legitimate, safe, beneficial research.

- **Risk experiments and studies are needed** to measure — rather than simply guesstimate — the health and environmental risks of different kinds of manipulations and releases of engineered organisms in different environments. Such experiments, which should accompany each new introduction, will demand, and may produce, a better understanding of the gene and ecosystem interactions into which the engineered genes are placed.

- **Agreements should be reached on who pays** for the consequences of any disaster with gene technology: the genetic equivalent of the "polluter pays" principle should be established.

- **Unbiased, investigative reporting** of developments as they evolve will be essential in establishing the right public awareness and regulatory framework for appropriate biotechnology.

RISK ASSESSMENT IS NOT EASY

Present risk assessment procedure for, say, a dangerous chemical, involves: identification of a possibly dangerous substance; assessment of effects of a given dose; estimate of likely exposure; and finally, detailing of the whole risk.

This approach could form a crude basis for risk assessment for the release of genetically engineered organisms, but difficulties arise because of:

- Lack of sufficient reliable data, particularly on long-term dangers.

- Entirely different types of risk, and experiments required to measure it, from one case to the next. Assessments on gene A in rice have nothing to do with those on gene B in rice or gene C in tilapia, etc.

- Difficulty in predicting the fate of released organisms or genes. Too little is known about gene and organism interactions.

- Secrecy associated with much private-interest genetic engineering.

- Absence of any monitoring procedure.

- Lack of researchers able or willing to make the assessments.

Hamdallah Zedan, the United Nations Environment Programme (UNEP) officer concerned with regulations on the release of genetically engineered organisms, argues that the first step towards quantitative risk assessment would be to conduct a detailed study of actual introductions of engineered species as they occur, to provide a bank of experience for later work and regulations. There is little sign yet of this occurring on any effective scale.

Unusual dangers

There are particular dangers that may be brought by the release of genetically engineered organisms.

Herbicide tolerance: Some people are concerned that a gene to protect a crop from a certain herbicide, to encourage farmers to use that particular product, could leak through natural crossing of the engineered plants with weedy species, into the weeds — resulting in super-hardy weeds that could not be destroyed with weed-killer.

But, argue proponents of the technique, such leakage would be very unlikely, as these species are very difficult to cross with agricultural crops even in the laboratory.

However, experiments are needed to show how great or small the risk is, say unbiased scientists working on the problem.

Insect resistance: As with herbicide resistance, it is conceivable that the genes for insecticidal toxins from *Bacillus thuringiensis* that have been engineered into crop plants to induce resistance to insects could cross into weeds, this time producing insect-resistant super-weeds.

Again, studies are needed to assess the crossing risk.

Virus resistance: The risks of introducing genes for viral coat-proteins into plants — to produce resistance to that virus — are that some other virus might collect that coat from the plant. The process is known as *transcapsulation*. That would give that virus the entry properties of that coat, so viruses might move into other crops than their usual hosts. However, this would not create a permanent new virus species, as the transcapsulated virus would not possess the genes needed to make its new coat; its new "entry properties" would last for only one infection.

In the other main method of inducing virus resistance — transferring genes of viral "satellites" that normally reduce the virulence of their partner viruses — there is a danger that mutations in the satellite DNA may induce the opposite effect: hypervirulence. This danger arises because some viral satellites do cause hypervirulence, and the real mechanisms of satellite action are unknown; thus it is not impossible (though unlikely) that one form of satellite could mutate into another.

So, says Dr Roger Hull, of the John Innes Institute, UK, "There should be an international research effort on the risks of non-conventional virus resistance techniques."

Marginal ecologies: Much "appropriate" biotechnology will be directed at marginal lands, in part because that is where the poorest communities live, in part because their land is needed to increase food production.

What effect, say, will a new engineered variety of rice, or some biopesticide, have in a marginal environment where the balance of creatures, soil and weather is delicate?

Some scientists are arguing that, for example, the Rockefeller Foundation (whose rice biotechnology programme is so well advanced) should encourage the development of national and international protocols to control and monitor the release of new engineered rice varieties, in case of environmental risks.

Live vaccinia vaccines: One of the most recommended — and most rejected — potential carriers for new vaccines is the vaccinia virus, the agent of cow-pox and in itself the very first vaccine. Vaccinia is so similar to the smallpox virus that it acts as a living vaccine against it, though it is much less virulent in humans and was used by WHO in the 1970s to eliminate smallpox from the globe.

Its attraction for use for new vaccines is that it can be easily engineered to contain the genes to express many extra proteins, which could be chosen to mimic and confer resistance to a host of other organisms.

But there are two risks. First, vaccinia itself causes a severe reaction in a minority of patients. Its use was justified in eliminating the more dangerous condition of smallpox, but would have to be reassessed for other diseases. Second, in wide-scale use, vaccinia might (the risk must be assessed) mutate to a smallpox form. If it did so mutate, now that smallpox has gone and youngsters are not vaccinated, an epidemic could arise.

Vaccinia vaccine proponents says the latter risk is very small and the former risk negligible and both are far outweighed by the potential benefits of the effective delivery of a vaccine, say, against malaria. But both risks clearly need independent assessment.

INTERNATIONAL REGULATIONS

An informal UNIDO/WHO/UNEP working group on biotechnological safety established in 1985-6 has been attending to issues of special interest to the developing countries in the release of genetically engineered organisms [5].

Individual UN organisations have also been developing their own guidelines, such as WHO's for the manufacture and preparation of vaccines in developing countries, or UNIDO's for the research work of its International Centre for Genetic Engineering and Biotechnology in Trieste and New Delhi.

Hamdallah Zedan of UNEP argues that, although genetic engineering has been in full swing in laboratories for over a decade, "the fact that no single health incident has been reported [at least, none has been proven]... could be attributed to the guidelines developed at that time". The guidelines — resulting from scientists warning of possible dangers — led to strict controls and containment of experiments. But as none of the vaunted dangers materialised, the guidelines have been relaxed.

At present, the general pattern in developing countries is that a group of scientists — without public representation — is defining regulations, leaving the system open to potential bias.

The most widely quoted existing basis for the international regulation of biotechnology is the report, "Recombinant DNA safety considerations" [6] published by the Organisation for Economic Co-operation and Development (which is effectively the rich nations' think-tank, and is most concerned about problems affecting those nations).

Nevertheless, on the scientific questions, the OECD advice can be taken as universal. On the release of genetically engineered organisms, a relatively novel issue in 1986, the OECD recommended:

- An independent review of the potential risks of any proposed release should be conducted, prior to release.

- The development of engineered organisms for release should move "step-wise" from laboratory, to growth chamber, to limited field testing and finally to large-scale field testing.

- Risks research should be encouraged.

- Meanwhile, the considerable existing data on the health and environmental effects of non-engineered organisms should be used to guide assessments of the effects of the release of engineered organisms.

FOCUS: Philippines fears lead to safety code

Heated public reaction to genetic studies on a rice fungus at the International Rice Research Institute (IRRI) in Los Baños, Philippines, has led to Presidential safety guidelines for biological experiments in the Philippines — the first such regulations in South-East Asia.

The guidelines, which were to be signed by President Corazon Aquino, are intended to control research and industrial work in genetically altered materials which could be considered to be potential pests or cause diseases in plants or animals, including humans.

Most scientists are relatively happy with the guidelines, which essentially leave control and judgment in their hands and do not provide sanctions for non-observers. Others, however, are worried that the guidelines will remain just that until they are given the force of law, with punishment for offenders.

Concern began in September 1987 when local scientists warned that IRRI was doing research — without appropriate containment and safety systems — on imported varieties of the rice fungus called "blast". It causes a serious disease which the Philippines rice crop has so far escaped.

The issue attracted such public attention that IRRI stopped the experiments. Genetic studies into the more virulent forms of the virus were delayed by two years.

"The programme for seeking permanent solutions to the disease has been set back," says Dr F. Bernardo, IRRI Director-General and a member of the committee that developed the new guidelines. But, he believes, once a national screening committee is established, and assesses the safety of the studies under the new guidelines, the research will be approved. And, in future, "if IRRI wants to continue its genetic studies on rice blast it will have to request approval".

Rice blast, caused by the fungus *Pyricularia oryzae*, is a major problem facing rice farmers in both tropical and temperate climates. The Philippines has been partially protected, because 70% of its rice fields are planted with IRRI-developed varieties which are resistant to blast fungus. But resistance usually breaks down after a few years because of mutation in the fungus into more damaging, or virulent, forms; IRRI was therefore investigating ways of strengthening and lengthening resistance by investigating these mutations.

IRRI began research into the genetics of blast virulence in 1986. No genetic engineering was involved. But the controversy arose because of the need in genetics to breed, and hence to let the fungus pass through stages in the greenhouse which produce the "seeds" of the fungus (spores) — which could escape if not sufficiently contained. IRRI had requested and received permission from the Bureau of Plant Industry to import selected spores. But it was stopped by public reaction when the work became known.

In Japan, Taiwan and South Korea, the experiments are conducted without special containment greenhouses. IRRI says its suspension of the project was only a response to community concerns, and it still maintains that the research is "not high risk". Even if the spores were to escape and germinate, the institute says, infection would be unlikely because the imported spores cannot infect local rice varieties.

However, the strength of public concern managed not only to halt blast fungus research, but also to lead to a ban on the import of radioactive gene probes (radioactively labelled pieces of DNA) used for gene mapping.

The new Biosafety Guidelines were drafted by the Department of Science and Technology and approved by the Science and Technology Co-ordinating Council. They call for the establishment of a National Committee on Biosafety (NCB), and for every research institution to create its in-house Institutional Biosafety Committee. The National Committee will formulate and review national policies, and will work with the government quarantine services in the evaluation, monitoring and review of projects. It will not have policing powers.

The guidelines do not "aim to regulate research, just the movement of organisms," says Dr William G. Padolina, vice-chancellor of the University of the Philippines at Los Baños. "They let you work with any organism as long as you know how to contain it, and you have the facilities... We didn't want to dictate what kind of work scientists will do."

He says: "A consensus was reached among working scientists."

But at least one scientist, Dr Benigno D. Peczon, will have no part in the consensus. Responding to Padolina's view that "self-regulation in research and development... is better than any imposed regulations", Peczon argues that self-regulation alone will not work: "We have to have laws, or else the guidelines will have no teeth," he says. What is more, he adds, inspectors "are paid so little money that the laboratories which are inspected pay the inspectors" — a situation unlikely to lead to independent reports.

Peczon also fears that private companies will not reveal much of their work to the NCB, despite its guarantees of secrecy: "Should there be private investors who are less than co-operative, or worse, less than ethically upright, does the NCB have any clout to determine what they are doing? Will compliance with the guidelines be mandatory or voluntary?"

CHAPTER 13

CONCLUSIONS

The impact of biotechnology on development is a complex issue, on which there may be many opinions. But as a guide through complexity, here are some suggested conclusions which the reader may like to argue for, or against:

- **Biotechnology is neither demon nor angel.** It should not be attacked as entirely a scourge of the poor, or as an unmitigated environmental disaster. Neither should it be uncritically embraced as a panacea, an instant provider of food, medicine and wealth.

- **The initial impact of biotechnology on development has been overstated...** Several early promises and threats — such as a malaria vaccine, or the swamping of the vegetable oils market with cloned palm oil — are failing to materialise.

- **But the delays in implementation are temporary.** From small beginnings in research, great economic and social changes are unfolding.

- **The diversity of biotechnology means no one will escape its effects, for good or ill.** Biotechnology is not the introduction of "a tractor" or "a dam" or even a simplified "high-yielding variety"; it is a growing set of techniques as potentially various as life itself, and it offers room for dealing appropriately with local constraints, crops and practices. Equally, it presents the danger that no one will be immune to the growth of biotechnology. Inappropriate, as well as appropriate, biotechnologies may impact every corner of developing economies.

- **One country's gain will often be another's loss.** And poor are at war with poor, as well as with rich nations. As this dossier reports, for example, China sold its hybrid rice technology to a Western buyer, excluding the rest of Asia from its success.

- **The key question is: biotechnology for whom?** Like any technology, biotechnologies are not neutral. They will be developed for the needs and purposes of the developer.

- **To be appropriate to a community, technological research should be directed by that community.** So for developing country poor, the goal must be the direct or indirect control of the development of the technology that will affect them.

- **The ball is currently in the donors' court.** The poor are hardly organised for controlling research. NGOs seem unprepared. The degree of enlightenment and concern, or otherwise, of researchers, donors, governments and private industry, together with familiar political and economic forces, will for the time being determine the equity or otherwise of biotechnologies that are developed.

- **At the same time, major efforts must be made to raise the level of effective awareness of affected communities.** Only very well-informed communities will be able seriously to influence research directions in their favour.

- **Biotechnology is mostly in private hands.** In practice, most of the tools of advanced biotechnology, particularly genetic engineering, are in the control of private multinational companies.

- **Multinational biotechnology will seek profit.** Long-term, potential profits in the South are seen to be large. Some technologies could bring profits to both South and North, but companies will not invest in such technologies unless returns are guaranteed.

- **Multinational profits demand markets and patents.** Profits will depend upon commercialising presently marginal rural areas. And with this, upon developing countries granting patent rights — a contentious issue, particularly where in many cases the patentable genetic material originated in developing country fields or forests.

- **Profit-seeking need not be entirely harmful to the poorest.** In this dossier, examples are given of multinational biotechnological activities in the South at both ends of the ethical scale.

- **Multinational research specifically in regard to the South is on a small scale** in relation to developments for Northern health and agricultural markets. The main danger may be the substitution of new Northern bio-industrial products for existing high-value Southern crops; the main benefit to the South may be some trickle-down technology transfer to groups working on more beneficial research programmes.

- **The multinationals are increasingly responsive to public**

pressure — which affects their market sales. Public information can again here influence events.

- **Public sector research is the real key to appropriate biotechnology.** In the context of private sector power, it is of paramount importance that public research on biotechnology for development is appropriate and well planned.

- **Researchers must "listen to the poor".** Short of adopting trickle-down theories of economic development, the only way to ensure the relief of poverty will be to listen to, respond to, and respect, the real needs of the poorest communities. Researchers must understand and learn from existing indigenous technologies, customs and constraints.

- **Such respectful interaction will be difficult.** The exercise of articulating real needs will not be easy. The extraordinary molecular sophistication of much biotechnology puts scientists at an enormous remove from the context of a rural village where the research might have an impact.

- **Field-to-laboratory communication is a matter for donors and NGOs.** Such long-range communication in biotechnology can hardly be managed by either end-user or scientist. It can only come about through effective, sensitive and imaginative field research, inquiry and communication. This should be managed by programme donors and governments in co-operation with those who know local problems — local groups and farmers, women and men, the poor as well as local elites.

- **The first solid benefits in agriculture** are likely to be the speeding-up of the breeding of improved crop varieties, and the early diagnosis of plant diseases for appropriate treatment and the control of epidemics. Later will come crops engineered for resistance to viral diseases, and to some insect pests.

- **The first solid benefits in health** are likely to be new tools of diagnosis, leading to faster, more appropriate treatment for individuals and better-informed health system planning. Later will come new and better drug treatments, and even later, vaccines against tropical diseases.

Biotechnology can be good for developing countries; but only if they and their friends make it so.

REFERENCES

Chapter 2

1. John W. Mellor, "Agricultural development opportunities for the 1990s — the role of research", address presented at International Centers' Week of the Consultative Group on International Agricultural Research, Washington DC, 4 November 1988.
2. International Food Policy Research Institute Report, 1987, p16.
3. M. Whitten and J. Oakeshott, "Modern biotechnology in the biological control of insect pests and weeds", paper commissioned for the Biotechnology Study Group meeting, 25-27 May 1989, Canberra, International Service for National Agricultural Research (ISNAR)/World Bank/AIDAIB/ACIAR.
4. Donald N. Duvick, "The romance of plant breeding and other myths", paper presented at the Staedler Genetics Symposium, University of Missouri, Columbia, MO, 13 March 1989.
5. As reference 1.
6. N.L. Innes, "Biotechnology and plant breeding", *AgBiotech News and Information*, 1989, Vol 1, pp27-32.
7. O'seun Ogunseitan, personal communication.
8. I. Manwan and M. Fatchurochim Masyhudi, "Rice biotechnology research program in Indonesia", paper presented at the 3rd Annual Meeting of the Rockefeller Foundation International Program on Rice Biotechnology, Columbia, MO, 8-10 March 1989.
9. Dr A.I. Robertson, University of Zimbabwe, personal communication.
10. Amarella Eastmond and Manuel L. Robert, "Advanced plant biotechnology in Mexico; A hope for the neglected?", Working Paper, International Labour Office, Geneva, March 1989.
11. Papers presented at the 3rd Annual Meeting of the Rockefeller Foundation's International Program on Rice Biotechnology, Columbia, MO, 8-10 March 1989.
12. "IRRI toward 2000 and beyond", International Rice Research Institute, Manila, 1989; "Implementing the strategy: Work Plan for 1990-1994", International Rice Research Institute, Manila, 1989.

Chapter 3

1. R.L.M. Pierik, *In vitro culture of higher plants*, Martinus Nijhoff Publishers, Dordrecht, 1987.
2. Bio/technology, June 1989, Vol 7, p548.
3. Max Rives, "Biotechnology and the Third World: The case of vegetables", in: *Plant Biotechnologies for Developing Countries*, CTA/FAO Symposium, Luxembourg, 26-30 June 1989.
4. Y. Demarly, "Technical aspects of plant biotechnologies", in: Plant Biotechnologies for Developing Countries, CTA/FAO Symposium, Luxembourg, 26-30 June 1989.
5. Albert Sasson, *Promises of Biotechnologies for Developing Countries; Agriculture, Food and Energy*, UNESCO, Paris, 1987.
6. As reference 5.
7. M.N. Normah, "In vitro studies and micropropagation of mangosteen", paper prepared for the Commonwealth Science Council, 27 June 1989.
8. As reference 5.
9. J. Farrington, "A review of developments in agricultural biotechnology and potential implications for the Third World", paper presented at an Overseas Development Institute Seminar, 11 May 1988.
10. Sinclair Mantell, "Recent Advances in Plant Biotechnology for Third World Countries", paper

presented at an Overseas Development Institute Seminar, 11 May 1988.

11. Tissue Culture for Crops Project, Progress Report, Colorado State University, Fort Collins, CO, 1987.

12. "Stress-tolerant sorghum regenerates identified in field trials", *Tissue Culture for Crops Project Newsletter*, Colorado State University, Fort Collins, CO, June 1989.

13. As reference 10.

14. As reference 10.

15. As reference 10.

16. Manuel F. Balandrin et al., "Natural plant chemicals: sources of industrial and medicinal materials", *Science*, 7 June 1985, Vol 228, pp1154-60.

17. E.C. Cocking, "Plant biotechnology; the way ahead", paper presented at the Annual Meeting of the British Association for the Advancement of Science, Oxford, 5-9 September 1988.

18. As reference 16.

19. As reference 16.

20. RAFI Communique, February 1987, p3.

21. R.H.V. Corley et al., "Abnormal flower development in oil palm clones", *Planter*, Kuala Lumpur, 1986, Vol 62, pp233-40.

22. "Tissue culture technology and development", *ATAS Bulletin*, November 1984, p16; Sinclair Mantell, as reference 10, pp3-4.

23. L.H. Jones, "Biotechnology in oil palm and coconut improvement", paper presented at the Biotechnology Study Project meeting in Canberra, 25-27 May 1989, International Service for National Agricultural Research/World Bank.

24. J. Dale, "Biotechnology in banana and plantain improvement", paper presented at the Biotechnology Study Project meeting in Canberra, 25-27 May 1989, International Service for National Agricultural Research/World Bank.

25. C. Teisson, "Biotechnologies for banana and plantain", Plant Biotechnologies for Developing Countries, CTA/FAO Symposium, Luxembourg, 26-30 June, 1989.

26. Gabrielle Persley (ed.), "Synthesis Report of the Biotechnology Study Project", presented at a meeting in Canberra, 25-27 May 1989, World Bank/International Service for National Agricultural Research.

27. As reference 25.

28. As reference 25.

Chapter 4

1. *Science*, 16 June 1989, Vol 244, p1293. This issue of Science has a special section on genetically engineered plants and animals.

2. Richard Walden, *Genetic Transformation in Plants*, Oxford University Press, 1988.

3. John Farrington (ed.), Agricultural Biotechnology: Prospects for the Third World, Overseas Development Institute, London, 1989, p50.

4. John Farrington, "A review of developments in agricultural biotechnology and potential implications for the Third World", paper presented at an Overseas Development Institute Seminar, 11 May 1988.

5. As reference 1.

6. As reference 5.

7. *Bio/technology*, October 1989, Vol 7, p1004.

8. H. Joos and W. Morrill, "Control of insect pests on rice using Bacillus thuringiensis genes", paper presented at the 3rd Annual Meeting of the Rockefeller Foundation's International Program on Rice Biotechnology, 8-10 March, Columbia, MO, 1989.

9. *Nature*, 12 November 1987, Vol 330, p160.

10. *Science*, 17 November 1989, Vol 246, p865.

11. R.N. Beachy and C.M. Fauquet, "Current status and future opportunities for the use of modern biotechnology in the control of plant virus diseases in developing countries", paper commissioned

for the Biotechnology Study Group meeting, 25-27 May 1989, Canberra, International Service for National Agricultural Research (ISNAR)/World Bank/AIDAIB/ACIAR.

12. C. Fauquet and R.N. Beachy, "Control of cassava viruses by in vitro genetic recombination", research project proposal for International Cassava-Trans Project (ICTP), 1987; W.M. Roca, "Cassava research problems and their biotechnology solutions", workshop paper, CTA/FAO Symposium, Plant Biotechnologies for Developing Countries, Luxembourg, 26-30 June 1989.

13. R.N. Beachy et al. "Characterization of the viruses associated with rice tungro disease", and R. Hull et al. "The molecular biology of rice tungro viruses", papers presented at the 3rd Annual Meeting of the Rockefeller Foundation International Program on Rice Biotechnology, Columbia, MO, 8-10 March 1989.

14. M. Wilson, "Plant viruses: a tool-box for genetic engineering and crop protection", paper presented at the British Association for the Advancement of Science Annual Meeting, 5-9 September 1988.

15. *Breeding for durable disease and pest resistance*, FAO, Rome, 1984.

16. As reference 4.

17. Steen Joffe and Martin Greeley, *The new plant biotechnologies and rural poverty in the Third World*, Institute of Development Studies, University of Sussex, Brighton, UK, October 1987; Rockefeller Foundation Annual Report, 1987, p27.

18. R.B. Singh, "Current status and future prospects of plant biotechnology in developing countries of Asia", in: Plant Biotechnologies for Developing Countries, CTA/FAO Symposium, Luxembourg, 26-30 June 1989, p43.

19. V. Walbot et al., "Expression of rice nuclear and mitochondrial genes", paper presented at the 3rd Annual Meeting of the Rockefeller Foundation International Program on Rice Biotechnology, Columbia, MO, 9-10 March 1989.

20. S. Day, "Switching off genes with antisense", *New Scientist*, 28 October 1989, pp50-55.

21. Charles S. Gasser and Robert T. Fraley, "Genetically engineering plants for crop improvement", *Science*, 16 June 1989, Vol 244, pp1293-99.

22. Kunisuke Tanaka, "Synthesis and accumulation of rice storage proteins", paper presented at the 3rd Annual Meeting of the Rockefeller Foundation International's Program on Rice Biotechnology, Columbia, MO, 8-10 March 1989.

23. Alice Y. Cheung, "Isolation of plant genes for carotenoid biosynthesis", paper presented at the 3rd Annual Meeting of the Rockefeller Foundation International's Program on Rice Biotechnology, Columbia, MO, 8-10 March 1989.

24. *Bio/technology*, September 1989, Vol 7, pp929-30; *New Scientist*, 11 November 1989, p24.

25. Gabrielle Persley (ed.), "Synthesis Report of the Biotechnology Study Project", presented at the Biotechnology Study Project meeting in Canberra, 25-27 May 1989, World Bank/International Service for National Agricultural Research.

Chapter 5

1. Gabrielle Persley (ed.), p26, "Synthesis Report of the Biotechnology Study Project", presented at the Biotechnology Study Project meeting in Canberra, 25-27 May 1989, International Service for National Agricultural Research/World Bank.

2. Bertram, "Biotechnology for cassava improvement", paper presented at the Biotechnology Study Project meeting in Canberra, 25-27 May 1989, International Service for National Agricultural Research/World Bank.

3. C. Fauquet and R.N. Beachy, "Control of cassava viruses by in vitro genetic recombination", research project proposal for International Cassava-Trans Project, 1987.

4. Albert Sasson, *Promises of Biotechnologies for Developing Countries; Agriculture, Food and Energy*, UNESCO, Paris, 1987, pp33-39.

5. W.M. Roca, "Cassava research problems and their biotechnology solutions", workshop paper, CTA/FAO Symposium, Plant Biotechnologies for Developing Countries, Luxembourg, 26-30 June 1989.

6. As reference 5.
7. C.M. Fauquet, personal communication.
8. As reference 3.
9. Steen Joffe and Martin Greeley, *The new plant biotechnologies and rural poverty in the Third World*, Institute of Development Studies, University of Sussex, Brighton, UK, October 1987.
10. J. Burley, "Applications of biotechnology in forestry and rural development", Commonwealth *Forestry Review*, 1987, Vol 66, pp357-67.
11. As reference 10.
12. As reference 10.
13. A. Francelet, "Biotechnology and the genetic improvement of trees", workshop paper, CTA/FAO Symposium, Plant Biotechnologies for Developing Countries, Luxembourg, 26-30 June 1989.
14. John Farrington, "A review of developments in agricultural biotechnology and potential implications for the Third World", paper presented at an Overseas Development Institute Seminar, 11 May 1988, p15.
15. *Bio/technology*, February 1987, Vol 5.
16. L.P. Mureithi and B.F. Makau, "Biotechnology and farm size in Kenya", International Labour Office, Geneva, 1989.

Chapter 6

1. Julia A. Walsh, *Establishing Health Priorities in the Developing World*, Adams Publishing Group Ltd., Boston, MA, 1988 (under the auspices of the United Nations Development Programme).
2. S.B.Halstead, J.A. Walsh and K.S. Warren, editors. *Good Health at low cost*, The Rockefeller Foundation, New York, 1985.
3. Julia A. Walsh and V. Ramalingaswami, *Biomedical Research Status and Opportunities*, Independent International Commission on Health Research for Development, Harvard School of Public Health, 1988.
4. As reference 1, p67.
5. E. Marshall, "NYU's malaria vaccine: orphan at birth?", *Science*, 4 February 1983, Vol 219, pp466-67.
6. Anthony Robbins and Phyllis Freeman, "Obstacles to developing vaccines for the Third World", *Scientific American*, November, 1988, p126.
7. Tropical Diseases: Progress in International Research 1987-88. Ninth Progress Report of the UNDP/World Bank/WHO Special Programme in Research and Training in Tropical Diseases, WHO, Geneva, 1989.
8. As reference 1, p85.
9. Cooperative Exploitation of the Phytochemical Resources of Developing Countries, work undertaken by Biotics Ltd for the Commission of the European Community, 1987.
10. As reference 3, p24.
11. As reference 1.
12. As reference 7.
13. *Science*, 10 November 1989, Vol 246, p747.
14. Barry R. Bloom and Aultony Cerami (eds.) *Biomedical Science and the Third World — Under the Volcano*, Annals of the New York Academy of Sciences Vol 569, 1990.

Chapter 7

1. *Bio/technology*, June 1989, Vol 7, p549.
2. H. Mahler, personal communication.
3. *The Scientist*, 11 December 1989, p1.
4. *Science*, 1 September 1989, Vol 245, pp903 & 973.

5. *Nature*, 28 September 1989, Vol 341, p323.
6. Tropical Diseases: Progress in International Research 1987-88. Ninth Progress Report of the UNDP/World Bank/WHO Special Programme in Research and Training in Tropical Diseases, WHO, Geneva, 1989.
7. K. Nordeen, personal communication.
8. Barry Bloom, personal communication.

Chapter 8

1. Peter Dart, "Biotechnology for agricultural microbiology", paper presented at the Biotechnology Study Project meeting in Canberra, 25-27 May 1989, International Service for National Agricultural Research/World Bank.
2. K. Jayaraman et al., Anna University, Madras, India, personal communication.
3. *Science*, 16 June 1989, Vol 244, pp1300-6.
4. As reference 1.
5. Steen Joffe and Martin Greeley, *The new plant biotechnologies and rural poverty in the Third World*, Institute of Development Studies, University of Sussex, Brighton, UK, October 1987.
6. As reference 3.
7. Albert Sasson, *Promises of Biotechnology for Developing Countries: Agriculture, Food and Energy*, UNESCO, Paris, 1987.
8. John Farrington, "A review of developments in agricultural biotechnology and potential implications for the Third World", paper presented at Overseas Development Institute Seminar, 11 May 1988, p14.
9. As reference 7, p34.
10. Gilbert U. Okereke, "Biotechnology to combat malnutrition in Nigeria", working paper, International Labour Office, Geneva, 1988.
11. *Science*, 11 September 1989, Vol 245, pp1187-89.
12. As reference 7, pp42 & 44.
13. *Science*, 16 June 1989, Vol 244, p1303.

Chapter 9

1. B.W.J. Mahy, *Recent Advances in Animal Biotechnology for Third World Countries*, AFRC Institute for Animal Health, UK, 1988.
2. John Farrington, "A review of developments in agricultural biotechnology and potential implications for the Third World", paper presented at Overseas Development Institute Seminar, 11 May 1988, .p41.
3. As reference 2, p13.
4. *Science*, 17 November 1989, Vol 246, pp876-77.
5. *New Scientist*, 9 September 1989, p42.
6. *The Scientist*, 27 November 1989, Vol 3, p8.
7. As reference 1.
8. R. Colwell, "Marine biotechnology and the developing countries", United Nations Industrial Development Organization (UNIDO), 1986.

Chapter 10

1. Gabrielle Persley (ed.), "Synthesis Report of the Biotechnology Study Project", World Bank/International Service for Agricultural Research, May 1989.

Chapter 11

1. I.R.M. May, *Science*, 1988 Vol 241, pp1441-9.
2. *Science*, 28 August 1987, Vol 237, p969.
3. Productive and Sustainable Exploitation of Plant Genetic Resources in Developing Countries, Biotics Ltd (University of Sussex Office), March 1988.
4. Cooperative Exploitation of the Phytochemical Resources of Developing Countries, report prepared for the European Commission by Biotics Ltd, 1987; *ICDA Seedling*, March 1988 (available from the International Coalition for Development Action).
5. RAFI Communique, July 1987, p5.

Chapter 12

1. M. Sussman et al. (eds), *The Release of Genetically Engineered Microorganisms*, Academic, London, 1988.
2. James M. Tiede et al., "The planned introduction of genetically engineered organisms: ecological considerations and recommendations", *Ecology*, April 1989, Vol 70, pp297-315.
3. "Deliberate Release of Genetically Modified Organisms to the Environment", submission of evidence to the Royal Commission on Environmental Pollution by the UK Genetics Forum, March 1989.
4. John Hodgson, *Scientific European*, April 1990.
5. Report of the 2nd Meeting of the UNIDO/WHO/UNEP Working Group on Biotechnology Safety, Paris, 15-17 December 1987.
6. Recombinant DNA Safety Considerations, OECD, Paris, 1986.

INDEX